The New Road

charting Scotland's inspirational communities

D1439794

Alf Young &
Ewan Young

ARGYLL ✠ PUBLISHING

© Alf Young & Ewan Young 2012

reprinted 2013

Argyll Publishing
Glendaruel
Argyll PA22 3AE

www.argyllpublishing.co.uk
www.centreforconfidence.co.uk
www.postcardsfromscotland.co.uk

The authors have asserted their moral rights.

British Library Cataloguing-in-Publication Data.

A catalogue record for this book is available from
the British Library.

ISBN 978 1 908931 07 8

Printing
Bell & Bain Ltd, Glasgow

CONTENTS

Introduction

THIS postcard from Scotland describes a journey round our country. Undertaken by a father and son, over eight consecutive days, in May 2012. We started in the small North Sea harbour town of Dunbar, east of Edinburgh, and ended up in the tiny village of Inverie on the isolated Knoydart peninsula, a boat-ride away from the west coast fishing port of Mallaig. We planned our tour as a journey of shared discovery.

Against a backdrop of nearly five years of financial crisis and economic stagnation across many of the economies of the developed west, we wanted to seek out communities, and individuals within communities, across Scotland, not content with waiting until politicians, central bankers and others in positions of power and authority eventually deliver on their oft-repeated promise to get us all back to something called normal.

What animated us was all the stories we'd heard of local initiatives beginning to challenge that orthodoxy. We wanted to learn lessons from pioneering people already charting new ways forward for their local communities. Ways that might define a new normal. Or even a range of new normals. A rich diversity of possible futures, fighting for breath amidst all the gloom.

We wanted to make our journey together because the troubled state we are all now in could, if it persists, begin to divide our generations. We were born in 1944 and 1982 respectively. One a representative of that baby-boomer generation, born at a time of great conflict, that tasted rationing, then reaped the benefits of decades of relative peace and rising prosperity. The other growing up in an age of digital wonder and easy travel, with two degrees and a year travelling the world behind him. Married, living and working in one of the most beautiful parts of Scotland, but now also part of a generation beset by doubts about what kind of world it is inheriting.

From the threat of climate change to the casualisation of work, from a broken housing ladder to one sovereign debt crisis after another, the storm clouds are swirling, in ways that are unprecedented in all our lifetimes. The social contract between our generations is at risk. Might a protracted period of public and private austerity after the years of debt-fuelled excess leave that contract looking even more threadbare than it already is?

It was the Irish-born philosopher, Edmund Burke, who first set out the terms of that deal in the late eighteenth century. 'The state is a partnership not only between those who are living, but between those who are living, those who are dead and those who are to be born,' he wrote. We must all now wonder whether Burke's contract between the generations can survive the twenty first century.

Alf grew up in a close-knit working-class family in Greenock. Four of them. First in a sub-let, a single room in someone else's small privately-rented tenement flat. Then in the basement of the same block, beside the coal cellars, with an outside toilet. He was the first member of his wider family to go to university. He became a secondary school teacher, then a college lecturer. After dabbling briefly in backroom politics in the late 1970s he found work as a journalist and remained there, mainly in newspapers, for the next thirty years. He is now semi-retired. Semi with a capital S. His wife and partner of more than thirty years is Carol Craig, series editor of these little books.

Ewan grew up in a nice old house in the village of Strathblane, north-west of Glasgow, in the lee of the Campsies, with Alf, Carol and their younger son, Jamie. Ewan has degrees in planning and environmental sustainability. He currently works as development officer for Ullapool Community Trust in Wester Ross. He is married to Merlin Planterose, who designs and makes her own range of silver jewellery. They live in a cabin they have built in a conifer forest overlooking Loch Broom.

So there you have it. Your two companions on this journey. One who started life in a cramped sub-let, now with the mortgage paid off and the pension intact. The other starting married life in a cabin, passionate about finding more sustainable ways in which we can all live our lives. What title might we come up with, to describe this journey? The image of a road loomed large. Not the road through post-cataclysm America described with such grim majesty by the novelist Cormac McCarthy. As a pointer to hope, despite all that has gone wrong these past five years, we finally settled on The New Road.

It's a title that's been used before, of course. Neil Munro first published his novel of that name, widely regarded as his most accomplished historical work, nearly a century ago. In 1914. Just as Europe was plunging into the Great War. Munro's tale of Highland intrigue is set in the 1730s, long before Edmund Burke had even laid out his concept of a binding social contract across the generations.

Its central device is the network of military roads built by General Wade into the Scottish Highlands in response to the Jacobite rising of 1715. Along that new road Munro's two central characters, Aeneas Macmaster and Ninian Campbell, travel north, becoming embroiled in the struggle between the traditional forces of arbitrary power in the Highlands and those seeking change.

The new road we traverse in the rest of this book covers some of the same territory as Munro's novel. However we cannot promise a re-run of the kind of escapades to which the fictional Aeneas and Ninian fall prey. That said, our new road is, like Munro's, firmly on the side of those trying to challenge old, increasingly-failed orthodoxies. We found much that was truly inspirational along the way. We hope you do too.

SATURDAY MAY 19
From the Dunbar Bakery
to Twechar Beach

WE PICKED up our new road in the town of Dunbar, East Lothian, birthplace of the pioneering nineteenth century conservationist John Muir. Muir died in 1914 and for much of the last century, while revered in California as the founder of the Sierra Club and a tireless campaigner, instrumental in the creation of the Yosemite and Sequoia National Parks, he was largely forgotten in the land from which his family emigrated when he was just eleven.

In 1867 Muir set out to walk a thousand miles from Indiana to Florida, seeking out the 'wildest, leafiest, and least trodden way I could find'. We had so much to do in the eight days we planned to spend together – visiting fifteen different community initiatives all across Scotland – that Muir's mode of travel was out of the question. It was to be trains, buses and ferries for us. And occasionally, when the vagaries of timetabling conspired against us, we even resorted to a car service provided by our series editor, Carol. Friends put us up along the way. And where that proved impossible we resorted to the cheapest hotels or boarding houses we could find.

11

We had spent that first Friday evening staying locally with our friend Zoe. Dunbar has had its ups and downs since Muir's time. In the early 1990s the townscape of this historic fishing port was looking rather run-down, shabby even. Property was cheap. But the pre-crash property boom, especially in Edinburgh, some 28 miles to the west, changed all that. Dunbar, on the main east coast rail line to London, became affordable commuter country for the capital. And here we were, on a sun-kissed Saturday morning, regretting the clothes we had packed, having coffee and macaroons in a stylish craft bakery and shop, on the High Street a block away from the house where Muir was born.

The place was buzzing. The artisan breads – one a wholemeal loaf using beer from the nearby Belhaven Brewery, another a Polish-style sourdough – fine cakes, pies and other savoury lines, and those delicious hand-made macaroons (three for £2.10), all made in the back, were being snapped up by a steady stream of customers. It's the lettering on the sage-green shopfront that offers the first big clue. Under a bare wooden board announcing in understated lower case 'the bakery dunbar', four more resonant words are painted onto the door lintel – 'the proprietor, the community'!

This community – Dunbar itself, the other main settlement, East Linton, and the patchwork of villages and hamlets that make up Ward 7 in the East Lothian Council area – now boasts a population of nearly 13,000, up 17 per cent in the past decade alone. It's thriving in simple numerical terms. But this community isn't prepared to leave the shape and success of its future together to chance or the decisions of others.

In spring 2008, it discovered the family-run bakery on

Dunbar's High Street was to close, because the last in generations of Smiths was retiring. Rather than wait for a branch of Greggs or some other big chain to move in, a group of locals decided to do something about it. Within a year they had researched and registered their community cooperative. The challenge of drumming up enough equity investors began. There have been set-backs. They couldn't agree a deal to take over the old Smith premises. Instead they signed a lease on the former Knox's newsagents across the street. That meant securing listed building consent to install ovens and all the ancillary equipment. And that required even more funding.

In October 2011, this community-owned bakery finally opened for business. When we were there its register of local shareholders had climbed to 482, subscribing a total of £45,000 so far. There's even an investor (with strong local connections) from across the Atlantic. John Muir would have raised his hat to that. The minimum equity stake is £20 and one of the perks is a 10 per cent discount on shop prices, though many investors choose not to redeem it.

After months of wrangling over whether this venture actually had community support, the bakery cooperative finally secured £53,000 of support from LEADER, part of the government's Scotland Rural Development Programme. When production finally started there were further problems finding bakers with the kind of craft skills the bakery needed. The steering group sought advice from Andrew Whitley, founder of a pioneering organic venture, The Village Bakery, in Melmerby, Cumbria in 1976. These days Whitley, a one-time BBC Russian Service producer, teaches artisan bread-making at his small-holding near West Linton in the Pentland Hills.

With help from him and the Bread and Roses artisan bakery in Northumberland, it's all beginning to come together at the Dunbar bakery.

It is now run by Ross Baxter, previous head pastry chef at Greywalls Hotel in Gullane. Ross was Scottish Patissier of the Year in 2011. So it's no secret where the inspiration for these popular French macaroons has come from. Ross has been joined by Pavel Broz, one his former colleagues at Greywalls, who has taken charge of the bakery's growing range of pies, quiches and other savouries, some with a Czech twist. And then there's 19 year old Natalie Helen, a newly trained artisan baker who has moved up from Leeds to take charge of the overnight shift, producing wholesome bread. Overall the bakery employs fifteen people, full and part-time. We met two of the youngest recruits, Darryl and Callum, local trainees brimming over with enthusiasm at the chance to master a real craft. Darryl couldn't find a job at all for the first two years after leaving school. Callum used to work in the bread section of the Asda supermarket, which opened in 2007 on the outskirts of Dunbar.

While the community bakery was our introduction to the new road Dunbar has chosen, it's only one of many initiatives beginning to re-energise this community. There are moves afoot to turn a second shop on High Street, Crunchy Carrot, which sells fruit, veg and wholefood staples, into another community-owned social enterprise. Many other initiatives are offshoots of Sustaining Dunbar, the local Community Development Trust. It started life in 2007 with a consultation exercise, knocking on doors and interviewing some 1500 local residents about their ideas and aspirations. We spent time with two of the people behind the Trust. Philip Revell, its project co-ordinator, is an engineer turned craft potter, who moved here from mid Wales 22 years ago. Janet Barnes sits on Sustaining Dunbar's board and is also involved with the management of the bakery. The original instincts of its founders were to explore what one small community could do to meet the challenges of climate change and peak oil. The Trust is currently in its second three-year period of funding through the Climate Challenge Fund.

Such issues are seldom far from public consciousness in this part of East Lothian. Just down the A1 sits the sprawling Lafarge quarry and cement works, one of Scotland's largest carbon emitters. And a little further on, down the coast, is Torness, one of Scotland's last two nuclear power stations, like Lafarge, French owned. There's a large landfill site and the prospect of an incinerator burning imported waste.

However East Lothian is already home to greener forms of electricity generation, in the shape of onshore wind farms. Aikengall, a 16 turbine installation, developed by Cheshire-based Community Windpower sits just under 10km southeast of Dunbar. Further west into the Lammermuir Hills is the much larger Crystal Rigg windfarm. Operated by Fred Olsen Renewables, it currently has 85 turbines. Despite its name, the owner of Aikengall is a commercial enterprise. It does however provide some community benefits and sponsorships and funds a BeGreen Shop, offering advice to local people on improving the energy efficiency of their homes. The shop, in West Port, shares a building with the Sustaining Dunbar offices. But Philip Revell says the Trust has much bigger ambitions on this front.

It has created a trading subsidiary to explore how the

Dunbar community could install wind generator capacity of its own, producing an income stream that would allow it to implement its recently-completed 2025 Local Resilience Action Plan. Revell and his colleagues have explored the feasibility of putting a single turbine on a local hill, provided they can find a willing landowner. A more ambitious proposal, by far, is to persuade the owners of Crystal Rigg, Fred Olsen Renewables, to increase their planned eleven-turbine third-phase expansion of that windfarm to eighteen units. Each of the seven additional units, publicly funded, would create a long-term revenue stream for each of the seven wards that make up the East Lothian council area.

It's a model we will encounter again and again on this journey. But it requires significant upfront investment by these communities or their council or other public bodies prepared to back them. Sustaining Dunbar's project co-ordinator is clear about why they have to think this big.

'The only way ambitious government community owned renewable energy targets will be met is through communities buying into large commercial developments,' he argues. 'And communities will need this income stream to invest in creating the relocalised, resilient, post-carbon infrastructure they will require to achieve government carbon reduction targets'.

Sustaining Dunbar aspires to do more than decarbonise its future, fight pollution and encourage more energy efficient homes. In an area long known as the Garden of Scotland, the Trust also wants to encourage more locally-sourced food, like the flour from Kirkcaldy which supplies its new bakery. And sitting beside the main east coast road south and astride the main railway line, it aspires to better-coordinated public transport options, a car sharing scheme and creating an environment where most young people can walk or cycle to school. Achieving that is also one part of its health and well-being agenda. And then there's that constant challenge in these fragile economic times – pursuing an enterprise and skills action plan that can cut down on commuting, train more of its young people in employable skills and help re-energise the local economy.

In March East Lothian Council opened a new community centre in Dunbar, named after the area it which it sits, Bleachingfield. This state-of-the-art centre incorporates the public library, halls for everything from dance to taekwondo, space for an after-school club, and a cafe area and kitchen which Sustaining Dunbar has successfully tendered to run. It will be run as a community cafe and kitchen. But it will also be used to train young people in new skills, along the lines of the community bakery. And, in an area once renowned for its fruit growing, we can expect it to be used to produce food too, starting with lines of preserves.

Outside there are reserved parking spaces for Dunbar's car club, Spare Wheels. Instead of local families investing in a second car, they are invited to join the club for just £25. Then they can book a car when they need it, from a seven-seater people carrier to a Mini, by the hour, day, weekend or week, at very competitive rates. There are three vehicles right now. More if the scheme really takes off. And for those who prefer pedal power there's a community bike workshop with trained mechanics to help you.

WE HAD tried to arrange a visit to a community-based enterprise in the Edinburgh area as our second visit of the day. However, as chance would have it, both Heart of Midlothian and Hibernian football clubs had made it to the final of the Scottish Cup, to be played at Hampden Park, Glasgow that same afternoon. We couldn't compete with an all-Edinburgh derby. So we had turned our thoughts elsewhere.

We made our way instead to the former mining village of Twechar, on the south bank of the Forth and Clyde Canal, halfway along its 35 mile length. They stopped producing coal in Twechar, which sits in open country between the towns of Kilsyth and Kirkintilloch, in 1968. That's when the Gartshore/Grayshill complex, to the south of the village, near the route of the main Glasgow/Edinburgh railway line, finally closed. Mining coal had been Twechar's historic purpose. This tight-knit community had grown in size for over a century, thanks to one local mining company, William Baird & Co. When the last coking coal seam closed, some of the local miners managed to find work over in Lanarkshire's remaining pits. But by the 1980s they too had closed. Despite some local industrial diversification into processed meat and cake production, times since have been hard. Its population fell steadily, bottoming out at 1300.

'Twechar is a pocket of rural deprivation in an area of relative affluence,' explains Sandra Sutton, a trained youth worker whose family roots locally run as deep as some of those colliery shafts. Sandra was the woman we had come to see. These days she's the driving force behind Twechar Community Action (TCA) and the Twechar Healthy Living and Enterprise Centre it runs.

The centre is easy to miss as you drive through Twechar from the canal bridge, heading south around the western flank of Bar Hill, site of the remains of an important Roman fort at the highest point on the line of the Antonine Wall. The centre was built in the early 1990s by the local council as the village's indoor recreation facility. It was badly designed. User charges deterred a lot of locals.

So, in 2000, East Dunbartonshire Council decided to close it down. Members of one regular user group, the local football team, Barhill Amateurs, were outraged. They barricaded themselves in and refused to budge. 'I was running a youth club in the school at the time because I couldn't afford this place,' explains Sandra Sutton. She had had her own brushes with officialdom. 'Years ago they shut down the school youth club,' she recalls. When, as a mother of three herself, she asked why, she was told, 'No youth worker will work with kids like these. They are out of control.'

When she invited them to train her, Sandra was told it needed a group of twelve to put on a course. So she found another eleven volunteers locally. All were trained. She became the school's youth worker. Now, with her own can-do attitude and the members of Barhill Amateurs occupying the recreation centre, an even bigger opportunity to win concessions from the council presented itself. A deal was eventually done. The following year the council gave the community a 25-year lease on the centre at a peppercorn rent. But there was a catch. There would be no contribution from the council towards running costs. Twechar could keep its centre. But it would have to find its own sources of funding.

Local people created Twechar Community Action, a charitable company, limited by guarantee. And managed to get Lottery money to hire someone, from outside the village, as community regeneration manager. But it didn't work out. Eighteen months on that manager left. The rest of the Lottery funding was withdrawn. With the centre looking as if it might, in Sandra's words, 'go down the tubes', she was asked to come in for six weeks to try and turn things round. Determinedly they managed to assemble fresh funding from a range of sources. The council relented and give them money annually towards core running costs. They also secured a grant from the Coalfields Regeneration Trust. It was enough to fund a major facelift for the building and pay Sandra's salary as replacement manager for the next three years. With support from a lot of volunteers, Twechar's mission became to turn its recreation centre into a genuine community hub. One that would cater for all ages, begin to tackle the employment challenge for local youngsters and become home to a range of village services that, up till then, were only available one or two bus rides away.

When we arrived that afternoon, a football match was in full swing outside. Barhill Amateurs, whose team had played such a pivotal part in saving the centre from closure, had just won promotion. That Saturday's game, open to anyone who had ever kicked a ball for the club, was to celebrate winning the league. When they clinched the title, the Barhill team had done their lap of honour round the village on the back of the truck normally used by TCA's environmental training project, a social enterprise that carries out landscaping and garden maintenance projects and trains local youngsters in horticultural skills. It's one small measure of how much Twechar's community spirit has been revived. Another is the way this poorly designed leisure centre, all slab walls and precious few windows, has been opened up to embrace its community. The zinc clad, double height glass entrance that was created in 2006 opens straight onto an airy community cafe.

That's where we first encountered Twechar Beach. On the cafe wall hangs a T-shirt with the legend 'I went to Twechar Beach and all I got was this lousy T Shirt.' When Twechar was still a colliery village and money was tight, miners who couldn't afford a family holiday would take their kids down to Twechar beach, an area of sandy ground beside the canal, for picnics. Now, on one Saturday each June, ten tonnes of sand are dumped beside the healthy living centre as the focal point for a community fun day.

There's a simple way to capture the rich array of community activities that now call Twechar's Healthy Living and Enterprise Centre home. Sandra shows us the room where referees get changed when Barhill Amateurs are playing at home. On Wednesday mornings it serves as the visiting GP's surgery. On Tuesdays it's the base for the local credit union. It also serves as an addiction advice centre. And a place where local people can get help with housing problems or financial advice. The main hall, big enough to house three badminton courts, and also indoor five-a-side football, other sports and social events. TCA has installed an air-source heat pump to cut down on heating bills and added photo-voltaic panels to further reduce the facility's carbon footprint. The centre rents out other space to a full-time village pharmacy. And offers rooms by the hour that will take from six people to forty.

Overall the centre is a hugely flexible space with foldaway furniture. A dedicated but failing recreation facility has been given a multi-purpose future. There are breakfast clubs, after school clubs and various other youth clubs. A daily mother and toddlers group. A weekly baby clinic. A lunch club. Prize bingo on a Tuesday. Guitar and drumming lessons for adults and youngsters. Zumba, cheerleading and cookery classes. Gym equipment. Computer courses. Even a recycling point for furniture people no longer want. One way or another, says Sandra, the centre now directly touches the lives of 1100 of the 1300 residents of Twechar, maybe even more.

It also provides work for 36 of them, in the cafe, as youth workers, in its environmental enterprise and elsewhere. Doing more to boost the confidence of local people, particularly school leavers, searching for work or training in difficult times, is critical to this Development Trust's mission. There's a board beside the cafe listing every job vacancy within fifteen miles and access to laptops and help with applications. There are three horticultural apprentices working with the environmental project and, to give some younger village kids the chance to earn extra pocket money, the centre now sends a van to Glasgow fruit market every Thursday morning. Paper runs are few and far between these days. The youngsters are paid to deliver a fresh fruit and veg run to those local residents who want it. And, since the produce is straight from the market, there's the prospect of a tip too.

'I'm motivated by the power of social change,' explains Sandra Sutton. 'It was instilled into me by my granny and my mammy that you have to help other folk.' Her time as centre manager extended to five years. These days she chairs Twechar Community Action's board, focussing, in a voluntary capacity, on bringing in funding and overseeing the centre's evolving development agenda. Money is an ongoing challenge. In the last financial year, turnover topped £500,000. But annual running costs are around £130,000. And with recession and austerity hitting income from meeting hires and catering, keeping things going financially doesn't get any easier. There aren't many sources of grant funding Twechar hasn't tapped since it started, from Regeneration Outcome Agreement Money, through the Climate Challenge Fund to, more recently, anti-sectarianism funding.

'Our aim is to bring in as much money from our own efforts as we can,' says Sandra. 'But we still need some grant support.' Ask her what's next and she focusses immediately on jobs and training. 'We'd like to be a proper training centre,' she says. 'The nearest college, Cumbernauld, is two buses away. If we could do more training here we could cut out the middle man and generate more income.'

For the first time in decades, new social housing is coming to Twechar. The old miners' rows are being demolished. The first 41 energy-efficient, mixed-tenure homes have already been built. Another 50 are promised next year. The total could eventually reach 200. That means more families coming to live in the village and more young people with hopes and dreams to be nourished. Judged against the achievements in its first eleven years, Twechar Community Action has earned its central place in shaping the next chapters of this village's heart-warming story.

From Diets to Huts: A Circuit of Fife

AFTER leaving Twechar, we spent Saturday evening in historic Culross, that gem of a village, tucked away round a headland from the Longannet coal-fired power station, on the north banks of the Firth of Forth, looking across to the nightly light show at the sprawling petro-chemical and docks complex at Grangemouth. The next morning Carol dropped us off at Inverkeithing railway station. Local bus services around Fife on Sundays, we had quickly discovered, are few and far between.

On another gloriously sunny day, our first stop was just along the coast at Burntisland, to meet Mike Small, founder of the Fife Diet. Mike, originally from Edinburgh, studied political philosophy at Birkbeck College, London and then did a degree in social ecology in Vermont, in the United States. He is an expert on another hugely influential Scot in the John Muir tradition – Patrick Geddes, the nineteenth century biologist and pioneering town planner. Since 2007 the Fife Diet has grown into a significant consumer network of people passionate about sourcing more of the food they eat from producers much nearer to where they live. When Mike Small came back from the US, he found work that matched his qualifications and interests hard to come by. He worked as a painter and decorator back in Edinburgh for a time. Then, having done some media training in the use of the internet and other digital innovations, he got a job with the BBC in Glasgow, in its growing new media department. 'It was good, but a bit boring after a while,' he recalls. He and his wife, Karen, were living in Dennistoun at the time, where they had their first son, Sorley. Mike was still restless. So, when the BBC started downsizing, he took up the opportunity of voluntary redundancy and the Small family moved to Burntisland.

Mike Small had already been contemplating doing something practical about turning the tide on the relentless globalisation of our food supply chains. Like both of us, he remains exasperated at that shocking story from 2006 about the UK-based seafood processor, Youngs. It announced a cut of 120 jobs from its plant in Annan, by exporting fresh shellfish caught off the shores of Scotland to Thailand for de-shelling, only for the packs of frozen scampi to then be air-freighted back into the freezer cabinets of UK supermarkets, a round-trip of some 12,000 miles. One of us, Ewan, lives near Ullapool where freezer trucks, waiting to load shellfish and crabs bound for the markets of Paris and Madrid, are a regular feature of harbour life.

So what action can local communities take to counter this entrenched and climate-threatening trend? Mike contacted a couple in Western Canada who had committed themselves to what they called their 100-mile diet for a year. This Vancouver-based couple, Alisa Smith and J B MacKinnon, later wrote a book about the experience, called *The 100-Mile Diet:*

A Year of Local Eating. The original idea had come about on a visit to their cabin in Northwestern British Columbia. [More on cabins later in our brief circuit of Fife.] Their food supplies for the trip were nearly exhausted. But they had dinner guests to feed. So they went out foraging to see what they could serve up. That meal of Dolly Varden trout, wild mushrooms, dandelion leaves, apples, sour cherries and rose hips, supplemented by potatoes and garlic from their cabin garden, so impressed their guests that, back in their Vancouver apartment, they decided to see if they could live for a year on food sourced from within a100-mile radius of their rented flat. Starting in March 2005, they jointly wrote about their experiences, alternating month by month, as the story unfolded. Initially their accounts appeared in an online magazine. When the book of their year was published, in March 2007, it hit the non-fiction best-seller lists. It even spawned a television mini-series.

Mike Small's wife had just given birth to their second son, Alex. Feeding two young children involves mashing a lot of foodstuffs up, so they embarked as a family on their own year-long experiment, starting in October 2007, to see whether they could eat food sourced from around where they lived in Fife, and to discover what that diet would feel like. They started a blog, chronicling their experiences, inviting others to follow the same localised diet for a year and share their achievements and exasperations through the blog.

Then they decided to try something on a larger scale. They invited people in their growing network to join them for a communal meal in the village hall in Falkland. On the menu were big pots of stovies, one with meat, the other a veggie version. When they got to the hall there were fifty or sixty people there. And, to their astonishment, so was a BBC television crew. STV would have been there too, but their crew had been diverted to Anstruther, to film Prince Charles eating fish and chips in the fishing port's award-winning takeaway. There had been no advance publicity about the Falkland meal. An inquisitive journalist had picked up on the story from the Smalls' blog.

'We had this extraordinary realisation that what we were doing was actually newsworthy,' recalls Mike. After all people had eaten meals together like this, cooked from local produce, for hundreds of years. But in a world of supermarket dominance, increasing food miles and seasonal produce available on demand all-year-round, what Mike and Karen were doing was striking a very resonant chord. Each time they held another meal, more and more people wanted to come.

Part of their rationale has always been strictly non-commercial, cooking for people to eat together, for free. As the network grew, other members volunteered to provide food and venues for the meals. Some local producers donated ingredients. The only funding the Smalls got in that first year was a small grant to provide creche facilities at the lunches. Mike believes a lot of families become quite politicised over food when they first have children, wanting only the best for their babies. So those early lunches, held all round Fife, were attracting a lot of couples with young children. That first grant, he says, stopped an emerging gender split. It tended to be women who signed up to the network. It still is. But at these early lunches the mothers were seeing to the needs of their children while the fathers stood around, in the centre of the room, debating the threat of climate change. A creche allowed equal participation in the debate that went with the food.

The Fife Diet, still being run from a bedroom in the Smalls' home, had developed real momentum and was getting noticed across the UK. It was beginning to garner awards, including one from the *Observer's* Food Monthly supplement. Its founders had to decide on their next steps.

'It had all been driven by our understanding of the realities of climate change from the start,' Mike explains. So when the Climate Challenge Fund (CCF) was launched in 2008, to help communities reduce their own carbon emissions, it was the perfect opportunity to take their initiative to a new level. Initially they got funding for a year, then for a further two years. Recently they won funding, under the scheme, for a further three years. But reliance on such grant funding can sometimes feel like 'a treadmill', he tells us, one that can, especially in times of austerity, sometimes threaten to disappear altogether.

In March, for instance, just before we met, Mike and his team were getting ready to wind the whole thing down. The packing cases had been ordered. Personal cvs were being dusted down. Then the new award, providing funding through to 2015, was confirmed. That means a network that is currently over 4400 strong, can go on growing. Mike Small expects it to hit 6000 in the next two years. So what kind of programmes does this CCF funding allow the Fife Diet to deliver to its members and promote among the disparate communities that make up this eastern corner of central Scotland?

In essence it seeks to encourage people to do six things:

- Eat local.

- Compost more.

- Waste less.

- Be more organic.

- Eat less meat.

- And grow some of their own food.

The Diet team surveys their progress, computes what that means in carbon savings and reports back on progress made.

'Thirty per cent of the UK's carbon footprint comes from the way we produce and distribute our food,' explains Small. 'The Scottish government aims for a 42 per cent reduction in overall emissions by 2020. We're in 2012, so that's a reduction of almost half in eight years. There's great ambition at a cross-party level, backing this. But, on the other hand, they don't really know how to do it.'

It's free to join the Fife Diet. For people embracing it, results so far suggest their carbon footprints from the way they choose to eat are, on average, 40-50 per cent lower than the footprint of the average UK citizen. The initiative's philosophy is not to tell people how they should go about it. Rather it's about offering suggestions and sharing experience, letting members find out what suits them and their family.

'It's about facilitating change?' Ewan suggested. Mike agreed. There are already two established organic producers in Fife – Bellfield and Pillars of Hercules. The Diet does suggest to new members that one easy way of getting started is to order a weekly veg box from one of them, tailored to each family's likes and dislikes, delivered to their door. It doesn't get involved in such transactions. But it does provide members with plenty of ideas about how to cook interesting and nutritious meals from scratch with that veg and soft fruit and other locally-sourced ingredients, like fish, meat, cheese and bakery products, all of which can also be delivered.

Apart from regular newsletters, members get a beginner's guide, seasonal recipe books, lists of local producers and a perpetual calendar, indicating what's available from season to season. There's also information on cookery workshops and other events. The recipes they promote are an engaging mix of the kind of food your granny used to cook and other ideas that would appeal to the most discriminating foodie.

But isn't this whole local agenda, with its emphasis on cooking each day from raw materials, just a bit onerous on hard-pressed, time-poor families? One Scottish journalist even suggested the Smalls, if they wanted to eat like this, should go and live in North Korea. Mike Small concedes there is something counter-intuitive in their approach.

'We are saying you're going to have less choice and that's going to be good for you.' But he insists it is not about ramming anything down anyone's throat. One of the core ideas behind the Fife Diet is what he calls the 80-20 concept. Instead of a diet where 80 per cent of what people eat can be sourced anywhere and regardless of season and only 20 per cent is sourced locally, he wants to flip that the other way round, with 80 per cent sourced locally and seasonally, leaving the other 20 per cent for the staples Fife could never sustainably produce. The Diet isn't suggesting members should give up on coffee, wine, chocolate, sugar or bananas. It's all about shifting the overall balance.

Full membership of the Fife Diet is restricted to residents of the kingdom. In such a diverse area, there are still communities it is trying to reach with its message. Each year it visits three new places, putting on events to show what Fife has to offer in terms of locally produced food and how membership can change the way families feed themselves in a more nourishing and ecologically sustainable way. With grant funding now assured for another three years, there's a chance to get off that treadmill and think about what other challenges the Fife Diet can now take on.

In the past year Mike Small and his five-strong part-time team have moved into space in all that remains of Burntisland's original railway station, opened in 1847 by the Edinburgh and Northern Railway. The old station house has been turned into a social enterprise centre and provides space for artists' studios. It's a historic site. In 1850 it became the northern terminal for the world's very first train ferry, linking Granton on the Edinburgh side of the Forth to Fife. It continued to operate that ferry until 1890 when the new Forth Bridge opened. So innovation is woven into the stones of these buildings, a good place to chart what's next for the Fife Diet.

In terms of its activities within the kingdom, Mike Small wants to build on Fife Council's supportive allotments policy by helping create a community food centre where any glut in production of vegetables and fruit can be gathered in and redistributed to families that can use it. There has also been a boom in new orchard plantings across the kingdom so, within a few years, there's a role to be played deciding what happens to all that produce too. Small can see his organisation becoming a co-op incubator unit to encourage new mutually beneficial collaborations.

'When we survey our members, they don't say they are doing this because of climate change, they say they want to know where their food's from. And they want to support local producers.'

The Fife Diet's success so far has been noticed well beyond Fife. It's already been copied by Speise Lokal, an initiative in Austria. There's Tipperary Diet. And one in Cornwall, another in Norwich. In Scotland, the Fife Diet has already launched Blasda (Gaelic for Taste) an annual celebration of local food movements and cultures throughout the country. From the Uists to Moffat, the Black Isle to Glasgow's Merchant City, things are happening. Funding support from the People's Postcode Lottery has allowed the Fife Diet to acquire a Seed Truck, powered by recycled chip fat, which is criss-crossing Scotland, helping other communites with advice and support about how to grow more of your own. How well and how far good ideas can travel is part of this story. When Mike Small contacted that couple in Vancouver about their 100-mile diet he discovered James MacKinnon's grandparents had emigrated from Cupar and would have eaten a Fife diet before that!

Finally there's the question of public policy on how we grow, consume and distribute food. The Scottish government is putting together a food and drink policy framework. As its contribution to the debate, the Fife Diet is developing its own food manifesto that goes well beyond anything any political party has so far promoted. Among its twenty key proposals, it wants a moratorium on supermarket expansion, a soda tax, one on plastic bags too, and a GM-free Scotland. It also proposes that no child should leave school without knowing how to make a pot of soup, a community right to grow, decentralisation of our food infrastructure, sustainable public procurement of food for schools and hospitals and other public services, farm apprenticeships and work experience through the creation of farm corps and garden corps. It's radical. It's challenging. It's a long way from celebrating because exports of Scotch whisky have hit another record high and the Chinese are now buying our salmon.

WE LEFT Mike Small – his two young sons peeking out from behind the stout stone columns that line the facade of the old station house to wave goodbye – and caught the next train to Cupar. We were off to meet two women who are members of a very different Fife-based network, one that is trying to address another of life's daunting challenges. Where and how people at the other end of the age spectrum from Sorley and Alex can most fulfillingly live out their later years. They call themselves Vivarium. And they think the answer to that question is for more of us, when we get older, to live in what some have called 'intentional community', in co-housing developments. One of the women who joined us for some lunch in Cupar described how the idea had first come up. Back in 2003, Clare du Boulay and two friends were talking over supper.

'We didn't really like any of the prospects facing us in our old age,' she recalls. 'Our pensions were poor. The thought of care homes, sheltered housing or knocking about alone in big houses didn't appeal. There had to be a better way.' They began to explore alternatives. That's how they found out about the concept of co-housing. 'It's difficult to get people to understand what co-housing is all about,' Clare complains. 'It's a difficult term. Some people say: Oh it's a commune. Others think you mean a gated community. I've now started saying it's a living group.'

Our other new acquaintance, Monika Holton, joined Vivarium later than Clare. She puts what they are trying to achieve another way. 'It's about a group of like-minded people with shared values deciding to live beside one another, preferably in as eco-friendly a manner as possible.'

Vivarium's quest has been a long one. From that original conversation back in 2003, the group started exploring what other options were out there. In 2005 it got Queen Margaret University College to produce a report on the potential for co-housing. Douglas Westwater from Community Enterprise Limited also produced a feasibility study including market research showing substantial interest in co-housing in the Fife area.

The following April two small groups from Vivarium travelled to Denmark and Holland to visit established co-housing projects and find out what 'living apart together' (another common characterisation of co-housing) actually feels like. From the beginning Vivarium was holding open meetings around Fife to discuss its progress. Others were getting involved. Membership of the network expanded. Vivarium currently has a steering group and up to 40 members. Though most live in Fife, membership is not confined to the kingdom. There are members from as far away as Edinburgh and Blairgowrie. The steering group are all volunteers although, thanks to a grant from the Tudor Trust, Vivarium did manage to fund a development officer post for two years, though that has now ended. In 2007 the Vivarium Trust sought and was granted charitable status. That requires it to promote education about co-housing, particularly the impacts, in terms of health and well-being, it could have on older people.

In March 2012, for instance, Vivarium took its case to MSPs in the Garden Lobby of the Scottish parliament in Edinburgh for three days. Charitable status also requires Vivarium to establish and support pilot projects which demonstrate and test the practical application of co-housing schemes. These are not easy times for anyone thinking of entering the housing market. Especially if the concept you are trying to drum up interest in is so seemingly at odds with Scotland's traditional approaches to housing its older citizens.

The original impetus for co-housing came in Denmark in the 1970s. Around 8 per cent of Danes over the age of 50 now live in such complexes. And there are over 200 more up and running across the Netherlands. Perhaps the best known there is the De Refter complex, a converted convent near Nijmegen which has been in existence for over thirty years. Co-housing is also a feature of the housing mix in the United States, Canada, Australia, New Zealand and Japan. Interest is also growing in England where, for example, a development of eco-homes built around the conversion of an old mill complex on the River Lune, near the village of Halton on the eastern outskirts of Lancaster, is nearing completion and fast selling out. Lancaster Cohousing is open to buyers of all ages. As well as your own home the complex offers, as a focal point for the community, a common house, complete with a shared kitchen, food store and eating area with guest bedrooms for visitors and a communal garden and terrace with views of the river. There is also a managed workspace where small businesses and social enterprises can take advantage of serviced workshops, offices and studios.

Vivarium has been talking to Kingdom, the pan Fife housing association, about creating a demonstration co-housing project in North East Fife, a development of between 20 and 30 homes capable of accommodating between 50 and 60 older people. The project would incorporate a common house, on the same principles as the one being built right now in that development outside Lancaster. It would be a new-build development, aimed at the over fifties. Further details, such as which other parties are involved in the development and the site that has been identified, remain confidential. But, according to Monika and Clare, hopes are rising that it is actually going to be built in the near future.

Unsurprisingly, both women have found the time it has

taken to get this far deeply frustrating. So we didn't press them for more details. They see the biggest barrier as making co-housing affordable. At present almost all existing developments have been funded privately.

With more people living longer, it's certainly time for some fresh thinking about how Scotland meets housing need, especially for older Scots. Though its journey, this far, has been a long one, Vivarium is no longer on its own in trying to promote new approaches. Of course the Findhorn Community on the Moray Firth is well-established and is now expanding again. And now there is a groundswell of interest in co-housing in other parts of Scotland, like Galloway and Selkirk. We can only hope that, by the time this book reaches you, Vivarium is watching its pilot project taking physical shape.

AFTER our meeting with Monika and Clare, we were picked up by our final contact of the day, Ninian Stuart, and driven back west to our final destination in Fife, the conservation burgh of Falkland, to talk about huts. For both of us this leg of our journey was laced with warm family memories. Thirty years before, when we were living in a large top-floor tenement flat near Glasgow's Botanic Gardens, the flat Ewan first grew up in, we bought one of the wooden holiday huts on the Carbeth estate in south-west Stirlingshire. Over the years the whole structure was virtually rebuilt, with a lot of help from Carol's Dad. We spent many relaxed family weekends there, preparing picnics and exploring the surrounding countryside. When Ewan was about to start primary school we decided to move out of Glasgow altogether and bought a very old and rather neglected house in the village of Strathblane, at the western end of the Campsies. Strathblane is just over the hill from Carbeth. Our hut was now just a couple of miles away. We could easily walk there. However our new home had a wild, neglected garden offering countless hours of exploration for Ewan and his younger brother, Jamie. So we sold our hut to someone who could make more use of it than we now could.

But huts have continued to feature strongly in our family story. In the 1990s we spent a number of holidays in Nova Scotia with Alf's cousin Arnold and his family. The Hudsons have a holiday cabin on the Gulf of the St Lawrence, near the township of Pugwash. We have spent many happy times there too. Finally since Ewan got married in 2007 and moved to Wester Ross, he and his wife Merlin have built another cabin as their first home, this time in a mature pine forest on the northern shores of Loch Broom, a few miles from Ullapool. Huts and cabins, and the pleasures they can bring, have helped shape both our lives. And when, as we were approaching Falkland, Ninian announced he was talking us to the Pillars of Hercules for a coffee, our memory-go-round was complete. We found ourselves sitting, in more warm sunshine, in the organic farm shop and cafe's orchard where, on an equally sunny day in September, nearly five years before, Ewan and

Merlin got married. That amazing wedding – bales of straw for seats; the open-air barbeque pit; guests bringing fresh seafood from the north to add to cuts of Merlin's grandfather's organic lamb on the coals; the joyous ceilidh – is now part of our family folklore. It was good to be back.

Ninian Crichton-Stuart, hereditary keeper of Falkland Palace, does not fit the off-the-shelf stereotype of a Scottish laird. He currently lives in a modest flat in the palace, completed in the sixteenth century, a main country residence of the Stuart kings and queens of Scotland for 200 years. It was one of Mary, Queen of Scots' favourite places. But the responsibility for care and management of the palace on behalf of the Crown was given in trust to the National Trust for Scotland by Ninian's father in 1952, before his son was even born. The rest of the 4000 acre Falkland estate, land that covers the ancient hunting grounds of these same Stuart kings and includes the nineteenth century House of Falkland, home to a school for boys on the autistic spectrum since the 1950s, is also held in trust.

Ninian, who prefers to be called plain Ninian Stuart says his father, who died when Ninian was 25, was concerned that his son's interest in community work and homelessness might lead him to neglect or even give away the estate. Ninian acknowledges his own ambivalence. He had grown up in the palace but gone to the village primary school. Whilst he inevitably found the palace grounds and hidden landscape exciting he also relished a normal village life with other local youngsters. When his parents sent him off to private school at the age of seven (Farleigh House, Hampshire, then Ample-forth in Yorkshire), things changed and his relationships with his peers would never be quite the same.

'I still feel very sad about that,' he says. But he did more than feel sorry for himself. In his late teens Ninian rebelled against his privileged upbringing and went off to Glasgow to become a community worker. He cleaned night shelters, worked with homeless women and in a therapeutic community and lived for four years (with his young family) in impoverished council estates like Ruchill.

He met and married a Glasgow girl, Anne Marie O'Donnell. They had a son and a daughter. He came back with his family to Falkland in 1990. But for another ten years after that Ninian continued with his community work, still in the mental health field, this time in Kirkcaldy. Then, in 2000, his wife died. As a trustee of the Falkland Estate Trust, his thoughts turned to the future of these lands. 'I got hooked into the idea of stewardship,' he explains. 'Looking after things that matter, but not just for ourselves.' That produced the Centre for Stewardship which has run the annual Big Tent festival in the estate grounds. The sixth Big Tent took place in July 2012. 'Its ethos is green. There's music. There's wide-ranging talk. And there's plenty of family fun.'

However we were on the Falkland Estate, at the Pillar of Hercules where, since 1983, Bruce Bennett has rented some twenty of its acres to establish his busy organic farm, shop and cafe, to talk about Ninian's latest campaign, to embed a widespread hutting culture across Scotland. He took us to see his own hut, more than a year in the building and still not finished, deep in the Chancefield Forest area of the estate. 'I'm phenomenally impractical,' Ninian concedes. 'But had A Thousand Huts not come along I would have finished this one before now.' A Thousand Huts is the campaign launched in June 2011 by the charity Reforesting Scotland, where Ninian is a director. Scotland lags way behind Norway, Sweden, Finland, Denmark, Russia and Canada in the proportion of its people who have access to a hut in the great outdoors.

The only survey that's been done suggests there are no more than 700 here and the owners of some of them have faced threats of eviction. One in 8 people in the Nordic countries have access to a hut. From that perspective getting another thousand huts built across Scotland over the next five years would still leave us trailing far behind. But it would be progress. Ninian has only himself to blame for campaigning when he could have been finishing the cladding on his own place. For it was he, at a Reforesting Scotland meeting, who got up on his soapbox and suggested the target of a thousand new huts in the first place.

He is drawn to the hut as a kind of spiritual place, a quiet retreat where the cares of modern life can be put aside and personal well-being fostered. His own mother had had mental health problems. 'Every so often life gets overwhelming and dealing with stress isn't easy,' he adds, reflecting on his own years of work in the field. 'You know I don't think anyone's totally mentally healthy.'

He himself was facing some difficult times towards the end of 2009. One important funder of the Centre for Stewardship had pulled out. Ninian was overstretching and had to take a step back. He found himself yearning for a hut of his own in the Falkland woods. He thought of going to B&Q for a flat-pack. But then he saw the potential of making good use of some of Falkland's mature supply of timber, and of fostering fragile skills that could turn that raw wood into structures of simple beauty. So while every visit to his unfinished hut was rewarding – 'The clarity of mind I found there was striking.' – he couldn't resist that soapbox.

'People got it immediately,' he remembers. 'The simple beauty and sustainability of the hut. The potential for building more with Scottish timber and rediscovering skills that might otherwise be lost. What we could do, in terms of hutters' rights, planning, building control and land ownership, to create greater access.' The campaign launch got a lot of publicity. A group called Nordic Horizons, using the theme 'Building Cabins and Building Character', took the issue to the Scottish parliament. The campaign's Facebook page is attracting more and more virtual hutters. Ninian has even been introduced to a website called Cabin Porn. 'Lousy name, great site,' he says. And so it is.

The Carbeth hutters have formed a community company to buy the land on which their huts stand. They have until 2013 to raise the £1.75m purchase price. There are plans to launch a Scottish Federation of Hutters. A number of land-owners, Ninian Stuart insists, are coming round to actively encouraging hutters onto their land. 'The first year,' he says, 'has been simply a time to share the dream and sow the seeds.' As he drove us back to Ladybank, to catch another train across the Tay Bridge to Dundee and onward to Stirling, our evening stopover, we all agreed that year two needs to see those seeds germinate into more huts on the ground.

From Wind to More Wind
by way of a Safe Govan Harbour

BY THE TIME our train from Dundee got there, our evening in Stirling proved a short one. Having checked in at the Golden Lion Hotel, we went for a curry at Mr Singh's, a restaurant we have enjoyed occasionally when our football team, Greenock Morton, played in the same league as Stirling Albion. Having eaten, we opted for an early night. Next morning Carol picked us up and took us to Fintry, a village we all know quite well. Lying in a valley on the northern side of the Campsies from Strathblane, it has had no public bus service for the past five years. There are buses to take pupils from this part of West Stirlingshire to and from high school in Balfron. That morning we passed the local one. It had broken down on the backroad from Kippen. A year after the bus service stopped, Fintry lost its post office and shop too.

But this community of 550 people, suddenly seven miles from its nearest shop, is extraordinarily resilient. It is home to a growing array of community initiatives. But it is most widely known as a pioneer in harnessing onshore wind power to create direct community benefits. Back in Dunbar and in

43

other aspirant communities, they talk about the Fintry model of how local people can invest in wind.

It all started in 2002 with four local men, known locally as the Fintry Four. Martin Turner, Bill Acton, David Howell and Gordon Cowtan had what Turner has called 'green aspirations'. He had spent time in Sweden as a youth where ground source heat pumps have serviced homes for thirty years or more. He once flooded Fintry's main street when drilling a borehole for his own heat pump by hitting an underground watercourse. Acton had tapped a hydro resource in his garden. The two of them were encouraged by the others to explore potential renewable energy sources that Fintry as a community could profitably exploit. For green reasons but also for the good of all. It can be a windy place. As an old milling centre it also had a history of exploiting water power. The evening they went to report back to the community council that, in their opinion, wind held the greatest potential, they discovered a commercial windfarm developer, headquartered in Italy, was also coming along to discuss plans for a 14-turbine installation on moorland east of – but out of sight of – the village. 'We thought,' Turner has recalled, 'why reinvent the wheel? Can't we just have one of theirs?'

It took years of at times tortuous negotiations but that's what they did. Or rather, Falck Renewables, the main developers of the Earlsburn 14-turbine windfarm, were persuaded to add a fifteenth unit to their plans. With strong community backing, FREE (Fintry Renewable Energy Enterprise) agreed to invest in the project and pay back the cost of that additional unit over fifteen years, receiving, in return, one-fifteenth of the farm's annual power output, throughout its 25 year generating life. To ensure the proceeds would be used for the good of the whole village community, a charitable parent company for FREE, the Fintry Development Trust, was created in 2007.

Nearly half the entire adult population of the village and surrounding area have chosen to be members of the Trust. By 2022, when the capital costs of their share of the wind farm are cleared, FDT is anticipating an annual income of up to £500,000 a year. Until then the income from the community's stake, after loan repayments have been met, will be much smaller. Up to £50,000 a year. And, as Fintry has discovered, wind is a variable energy source. In one recent eighteen-month period, their investment in Earlsburn generated virtually no surplus at all. So at this stage, when deciding how the income is to be spent on community-wide initiatives, it's important not to simply spend what you earn, but to build up reserves that can be used when the wind doesn't blow so much.

You have to drive out of the village on the B822 as far as Waterhead Farm, to get a proper view of the Earlsburn array. Walk up closer and you'd think the community owned just one of the turbines. The bottom of its column is covered in greetings messages, penned by villagers. They date from launch day and were supposed to symbolise Fintry's one-fifteenth share. Unfortunately the wipe-off markers they used turned out to be indelible. But for the lasting impact of this pioneering deal on this small Stirlingshire community, you have to go back to the village and see how its creative embrace of the turbines on its doorstep is helping Fintry achieve its dream of becoming what the Trust's project manager, Kelly

McIntyre, describes as a 'zero waste, zero carbon, sustainable community'.

Fintry is not on mains gas. Traditionally villagers have used oil, LPG or even coal to heat their homes. Not very green options. And, as the price of heating oil has soared, increasingly costly too. At first the Trust set out to discover the extent of fuel poverty in the village. Nearly half the households were spending more than 10 per cent of their income on fuel, the accepted definition. Using some of the first income from the wind turbine, support from a major electricity supplier and money from the government's Climate Challenge Fund, FDT launched a major insulation programme. Three-quarters of the 330 households in the community actively took part. Of those 61 per cent were able to benefit from the free insulation on offer. Fuel poverty was cut by a quarter. And Fintry's carbon footprint began to shrink accordingly.

The Trust wasn't going to stop there. As the revenues from the Earlsburn wind farm continued to come in, it has employed two energy advisors. In June 2011 it launched its own grant scheme, offering financial support of up to £500 per household towards everything from the cost of installing greener heating systems to improving insulation and glazing. In its first year of operation 43 grants were approved. Fintry is well on the way to becoming the heat pump capital of Scotland, we're told, but all other renewable technologies and even wood-burning stoves are eligible for support. The Trust has also helped an earlier community initiative, the Fintry Sports and Recreation Club, to install a commercial biomass boiler. The club, founded in 1989 on land gifted to the community, now boasts a fully equipped gym, a four-rink indoor bowling green, two squash courts, a sauna and rugby and football pitches. It's also home to an annual music festival which attracts large audiences to hear musicians of the calibre of Eddi Reader and the Treacherous Orchestra.

Away from the sporting facilities, it also provides office space for the FDT. With its own membership of around 750, the sports club is testimony to the resilience of another group of local people. People like Sandy Kelso who was one of Ewan's teachers at Balfron High School. When the shop and post office closed down in 2008, a rota of volunteers started driving daily to Balfron to pick up newspapers, milk and bread. Now the club has cemented its place as the village hub by finding space for a replacement shop, providing newspapers and magazines and a range of basic groceries. And a mobile post office visits the club car park twice a week.

In Fintry, community resilience doesn't stop there, with the Development Trust and the sports club. The latter boasts a bar that serves food all day. However, when the other village pub on the main street looked like closing too, a third group of local people got together to purchase it and reopen it as a community interest company. FDT has collaborated with the Sports Club to plant a 40-tree community orchard around the perimeter of the playing fields. When the trees mature the fruit will be available for locals to pick. Additional space has been identified for allotments. And across the road at the village primary school, where another seven fruit trees have been planted, the Trust has invested in a green classroom, an outdoor space leading on to open fields where the youngsters of the village can learn more about the natural world in which their community is set.

We also discovered that, like Dunbar, Fintry launched FEET (Fintry Energy Efficient Transport), the village's own community car club, in 2011. It had two vehicles while we were there, popular for short shopping trips to Killearn or Lennoxtown, even persuading some two-car households to downsize to one. Since then they have trialled a third, electric car.

One big question remains. If all goes to plan and the wind keeps blowing, what will Fintry do with community income of up to half a million pounds a year when it has paid off its share of Earlsburn in ten years time? Gordon Cowtan, one of the original Fintry Four, lets us in on some of the Trust's long-term thinking. The buildings at the primary school are showing their age. Given the growing pressures on council budgets, promised replacement dates keep slipping. Might they eventually build their own primary school and lease it back to the local authority? Or might they consider investing in a care home within the village where Fintry's older residents might live out their lives in familiar surroundings? It looks as if harnessing their share of the winds that blow across the Campsies is enabling the people of Fintry to think right out of the box when it comes to trying to shape their collective destiny.

WITH no bus to take us on to our next visit, Carol came back and drove us into Glasgow and across the Clyde to a very different kind of initiative. In Govan. One that tries to re-ignite a spark of self-esteem in some of the most damaged and deprived people anywhere in Scotland. Gehan Macleod, the woman who runs GalGael, describes it as a 'safe harbour'. A bit of shelter from the storms, that batter the lives of those living with worklessness, from families where unemployment spans the generations. Emotional storms like depression or anxiety. Or whose lives have been scarred by alcohol or drug abuse. And offenders emerging from prison. But not a haven for the lost and the helpless that demands nothing in return from those who cross its threshold.

GalGael's workshop in Fairley Street is a clamorous place where those who join its community are expected to learn new skills and make things, notably wooden boats, like birlinns, the traditional Hebridean longboats of old. This is a place driven by a deceptively simple belief. That only by imparting a sense of practical purpose in those who come its way, can the fractures in their lives be healed. The word GalGael is drawn from the name of a ninth century people, the Gal Gaidheal, a genetic melding of the Norse and the Gael which helped shape Scotland's story. 'There is a bit of the stranger and a bit of the native in us all,' suggests the charity's website. It's an inspiring place where the visitor quickly learns to expect the unexpected.

Govan

49

Alf had been here before, with Carol. Ewan was making his first visit. As we arrived we spotted one of GalGael's founding directors, the writer and local resident, Alastair MacIntosh, walking along the street with another group of visitors. They turned out to be Papuan regional planners from Indonesia, at the start of a Scottish study tour that would, fortuitously, bring us all together again later that same week. It's not the kind of encounter you'd expect just a stone's throw from Ibrox, home of the by then deeply-troubled Rangers Football Club. But it's exactly what you'd expect whenever Alastair's around.

The founder of the Centre for Human Ecology decided, once we'd all met up with Gehan, to hold an impromptu seminar in GalGael's reception area, observed by a portrait of its bearded founder and inspiration, Colin Macleod, beneath a swooping eagle carved from solid wood. With the help of a translator, Gehan described GalGael's history and mission while Ewan and I explained the road we were travelling and why we'd chosen it.

The man whose painted image was looking down on us would have revelled in our chance exchanges. Colin Murdo Macleod was born in Australia in 1966 to parents of Hebridean and Irish descent. When Colin was four his family returned to Scotland and settled in the Pollok housing scheme in south-west Glasgow. That quadrant of the city, with Govan on the southern bank of the River Clyde at its heart, had been a magnet for Gaelic and Irish labour in the heyday of Glasgow's evolution into a great industrial city. In just a couple of generations Govan's population soared from 3000 to 90,000. In this part of Glasgow back then, most households were bilingual. A large part of the attraction the city held for them was its maritime tradition. It built ships, lots of ships. And through the maritime trade its merchants traded with the rest of the world. But in the latter half of the twentieth century that *raison d'être* was already unravelling.

The Macleod family came back to a Clydeside hit by mounting shipyard closures and rationalisations culminating in the famous work-in, led by a group of young shop stewards including Jimmy Reid and Jimmy Airlie. One by one the docks were falling silent. By the time Colin left school, in 1983, what was left of shipbuilding had been nationalised but was still struggling to win anything other than naval orders. Trade was becoming containerised and moving to new and bigger ports, mostly on the eastern seaboard of the British Isles. Locally apprenticeships were drying up. Rising joblessness stalked these communities. The blame was heaped on one politician's head, that of the then prime minister Margaret Thatcher.

Young Colin didn't thrive at school. He was, self-confessedly, a bit of a tearaway. 'Scratch the surface and I was one of those neds . . . running about daft,' he once told the BBC. But living beside the great parkland of the Pollok Estate, he was also able to pursue something that did interest him hugely – wildlife and exploring the wonders of the natural world on his doorstep. While running around with the lads, he also discovered an aptitude for bringing some sense of order to the lives of some of them. And, with an instinctive sense of the importance of community, he was trying to make sense of what was happening to the places and people around him, where meaningful work and aspiration were drying up, giving way to a sense of dependency, hopelessness and ultimately alienation.

His parents persuaded Colin to go away and train to be a forester and, when he came back to the city, he worked as a tree surgeon for a time. Then he started travelling – to Russia and then to North America – where he spent time with Native Americans, notably the Lakota Sioux people of South Dakota. He learned of their struggles to preserve the best of their culture and identity. And he began to learn how to carve in wood and stone. When he returned to Glasgow plans were being formulated to drive a new section of the M77 motorway throughout his beloved Pollok Park. In 1995 he launched a direct action campaign to stop the road's progress. The Pollok Free State was born. Colin even spent nine days living in a giant beech tree, scheduled by the motorway contractors for felling. The media immediately dubbed him the Birdman of Pollok.

The struggle to stop the motorway was lost. But within two years Colin had used his new-found public profile to launch the GalGael Trust, his vehicle for giving the young and dispossessed of Govan fresh hope. It was more a creative, learning community than a conventional training programme. It called the twelve-week experience it offered – a mix of craft skills and field trips – Navigate Life. Some dismissed it as 'back-to-nature mysticism'. To which Colin would retort: 'I'm the most practical person you'd ever meet'.

Then, at the height of his powers, the inspirational leader of the GalGael community died. He was just 39. He left the woman he had met and married during the Pollok Free State occupation a widow with three young children. But Gehan

Macleod picked up Colin's torch and runs GalGael to this day. Seven years on, she still has many of the same team around her, people like Tam McGarvey who oversees the learning – the navigation, if you like – and the redoubtable Helen Hollywood, who runs the office. Like Colin they wrestle, week in, week out, to anchor their great dream in reality.

'We've got all this raw potential,' explains Gehan. 'We've got machinery and a workshop. We've got product. We've got a brand. We've got committed people and we've got ideas. But the way things are with funding right now, to pull it all together, we've got to generate more income.'

During our brief sojourn in Fairley Street some people were still making boats. One man showed us his latest creation, what older generations of Scots would have called a kist. Another was taking old whisky barrels apart and turning them into decorative tiles. Someone else was carving designs on a bespoke set of garden furniture. On the metalworking side they make security grills for shops. And, out the back, capitalising on last winter's fallen tree harvest, they've started a wholesale logs initiative.

Navigating the tick-box culture which dominates so much of what's left of grant funding and charting a sustainable course through the choppy waters of welfare reform throws up other challenges. GalGael draws strength from its deep community roots. Every Thursday evening it's open house when those who have been involved in any way with this remarkable venture can come in, talk, do some work, make music and share some food.

There's even a four-verse GalGael grace that captures that sense of community better than any words we could write.

> We're cast into a crazy world
> Wi' many a sore disgrace
> Where greed o'turns compassion
> And respect is laid to waste
>
> Nae wonder then I linger here
> Wi' brethren mare distinguished
> Whose grasp on human kindness
> Will never be relinquished
>
> And share a cup and gie a hand
> Tae those who share this greeting
> To be a kent face and earn a place
> At GalGael's weekly meeting
>
> So before we eat, let's all think weel
> On the value of this clan
> That feeds our bodies, hearts and minds
> To help us make our stand.

WHAT we had experienced in Fintry and Fairley Street could not have thrown up more of a contrast. But what we were about to discover at our final community initiative of the day would add another rich layer of complexity to the texture of our new road. We took the subway from Copland Road back into St Enoch and walked to Central Station. Next a train to Neilston, tucked away in the east Renfrewshire hills, at the end of one of Glasgow's southern suburban rail lines.

Historically this was a community built on cotton. Where Govan built ships, the mills around the village of Neilston spun cotton, bleached, dyed and printed the resultant cloth and churned out vast quantities of thread too. They say that, in the trade's heyday, from source to where it joins the River Cart back in the city, the valley of the local River Levern was the most industrialised stretch of water anywhere in Scotland.

The mills have gone the way of the shipyards, though one massive complex, Crofthead, one of the oldest mill sites in Scotland which finally closed in 1992, still stands. The first clue to what was next for Neilston came at Patterton, the stop before our destination. It was four on a very hot afternoon. The carriages were suddenly crammed with pupils from Eastwood High School, heading home to the trim modern housing estates that soon came into view encircling what's left of the old village. With a population now over 6000, Neilston is a fast growing commuter village, popular with

Neilston

families that enjoy its rural feel but mostly find work twelve miles away in Glasgow or beyond.

The people who have persuaded this community to rethink its future were not initially driven by the eco concerns of the Fintry Four or the civic subversiveness of a Colin Macleod. But, in their drive to deliver a Neilston renaissance, they have already invested more heavily in wind power than their Campsie cousins and, along the way, have bought a bank. The story of how the Neilston Development Trust came to be is full of fresh surprises.

Pauline Gallacher, the moving spirit behind NDT, has lived in the village all her married life. We met her in the Trust's bank, or rather in the fine, refurbished sandstone building that used to house the last bank in Neilston, a branch of the Clydesdale. When its closure was announced in late 2005, the community tried to stop the loss of an important local amenity. When that failed, Pauline persuaded a group of like-minded villagers to use the community right to buy provisions of the Land Reform (Scotland) Act 2003 to acquire the building outright.

'This was not in our plans,' she recalls. From 2003, thanks to a NESTA scholarship, Pauline had been exploring how her home village worked spatially and socially and how grassroots initiatives might change it for the better. 'Conventional physical regeneration doesn't work because it's all top-down and prescriptive,' she argues.

Having studied art history, planning and, later, architecture, she had worked in community-based housing associations and was initiatives director for Glasgow 1999, City of

Architecture and Design. Now she was bringing her professional knowledge of place-making to bear on what the future
might hold for her own village. Through a series of public
meetings and participation events, she got other residents to
start thinking about how Neilston might be reinvented. An
annual Neilston Live cultural festival was launched. Pauline
called her original project Space to Live. Launched in 2004,
it tapped into professional and academic expertise in
Scotland. By the time Clydesdale decided to close its bank
branch, it had even held an international workshop, led by
the office of Jan Gehl, the renowned Danish architect and
urban design consultant. Gehl's philosophy – 'First life, then
spaces, then buildings – the other way round never works.' –
echoes Pauline Gallacher's own approach to successful place-
making.

So buying a bank – or any other building – at this stage,
was not in the plans. But, with the Clydesdale gone, this
landmark presence on Neilston's Main Street would be sold
anyway. Using the 2003 legislation to bring it under
community control would make a big statement. When their
letter of intent was lodged, on Burns Day 2006, they
discovered the building was already on the market. The
process thereafter was far from easy. Their target was primarily
a commercial building, not a piece of land needing reform.
The community had to show its support through voting for
the purchase in sufficient numbers in a three-day ballot.
Funding support had to be secured, with the Big Lottery
eventually backing the bid. The whole transaction took nearly
a year out of Pauline's life.

But, on St Andrew's Day, the keys were finally theirs.

Neilston was only the fourth community in Scotland to take the right-to-buy process through to completion, the first to show it could be used to acquire what was essentially a commercial building. To facilitate the deal, Space to Live had given way to the new Neilston Development Trust. The following year, after initial repairs and the installation of a kitchen, the bank reopened as a community cafe and resource and as a base for the new Trust, still run, as the earlier initiative had been, on a voluntary basis by Pauline and her small team.

Buying the bank had been a diversion. But the core work of fleshing out a clear vision for the future of Neilston was also proceeding apace. Crucially East Renfrewshire Council was persuaded to back this bottom-up regeneration process. A town team, chaired by a local councillor, serviced by council staff, expanded and deepened the community buy-in. After five years thinking and talking about the village's future, in June 2009 the Neilston Renaissance Town Charter was agreed and published. It lists 44 projects, from quick wins to long term aspirations, diverse in scale and cost, all meticulously prioritised.

'It's a document of the people, by the people,' says Pauline. Clearly, if the charter's aims were all to be delivered by the target date of 2030, it could help rewrite fundamentally how we do local regeneration, even how we do local democracy, in Scotland.

The big outstanding issue, getting tougher all the time after the 2008 banking crash and subsequent recession, is resources. The price tag attached to the projects in the charter totalled upwards of £15m. How might a village the size of Neilston come up with that kind of money? Neilston

Development Trust was continuing to develop the bank as its shop window but knew the building, to achieve its full potential, would require a further expensive upgrade. Even then there was no possibility of it generating a big enough surplus to finance the shopping list of projects in the charter.

Pauline and her colleagues were aware of the Fintry model of harnessing wind power. They had thought of attempting a Fintry-style buy-in to Scottish Power's Whitelee windfarm, one of the biggest in Europe. Then the opportunity arose to do a different kind of deal. A Stirling and London-based commercial enterprise, Carbon Free Developments, was looking at a four-turbine array on brownfield land 4km south of the village, at the old Drumgrain landfill site. Carbon Free specialises in smaller onshore windfarms where the local community is actively encouraged to get involved on a full joint venture basis. So the Neilston Community Windfarm was born.

The Trust was initially offered a 49.4 per cent share. It eventually settled for a 28.3 per cent stake, its purchase funded by loans from a range of social enterprise investors. The Trust worked hard to win community support for the deal. There was opposition from the smaller settlement of Uplawmoor, closer to the Drumgrain site, but shielded from it by a ridge. Planning permission was granted, by a whisker, in May 2011. The £15.6m 10MW windfarm will come on stream early in 2013. The community has been promised a return of around £10m from its investment over the life of the turbines, the bulk of it accruing after 2018, when those loans have been redeemed. That's up to £500,000 a year, which looks impressive when compared with the £100,000 cash a year which is East Renfrewshire's share in community benefits, from the much larger Whitelee array.

Meanwhile the Trust's bank has had its £700,000 upgrade, supported by eleven different funders. It reopened in December 2011, a bright and airy space any community would be proud to own. The annual festival has gone from strength to strength, supplemented by Go Neilston, a programme of walking and cycling events. There's been a local conversation with all the village over-60s about their aspirations. A two-year Powerdown progamme, aimed at helping local people reduce their own carbon footprint, brought some assistance to around a thousand residents. Among the bigger ambitions still to be realised is what can be done to restore and regenerate the now overgrown and neglected grounds of Cowden Hall, home to the owners of the Crofthead Mill. The house is long gone. The grounds are still a popular spot for dog walkers. But older residents remember the extensive formal gardens that have now grown wild. Might it be possible to bring them back to something approaching their former splendour? There are certainly precedents for that and the impact such restoration can have on a local economy.

Ewan's younger brother Jamie, who has just completed a two year traineeship at the National Trust for Scotland's Inverewe Gardens in Wester Ross has now moved to Cornwall to work at the Lost Gardens of Heligan, which a group of enthusiasts brought back to life after nearly a century of decline. Their leader was Tim Smit, the music producer turned social entrepreneur, who went on to create the world famous Eden Project nearby. Together these two garden projects have helped transform the fortunes of that part of Cornwall. Neilston take note. Now that your renaissance plans are agreed and your funding stream looks assured, it's time to make some of your big dreams come true.

Monday had been a long but exhilarating day. The early evening sun was still beating down as we took the train back to Glasgow and treated ourselves to a taxi out to the west end, where our friend Jean had promised us both a bed for the night. She had even cooked us a wholesome stew. And brought us news that her son, Colin, and his BBC production team, had taken a Bafta for their factual series about soldiers, *Our War*.

From the Turkey Red Vale
to Nissen Huts in Perthshire

NEXT MORNING, breakfasted, we walked down to Hyndland railway station to catch our train. This time on the Balloch line, to what the man waiting to meet us calls The Renton. That definite article really matters. There was a time when this former industrial village on the west bank of the River Leven was numbered among the most acutely deprived communities in Scotland. A failure on almost any index of poverty that has ever been computed, a community where hope had gone. It had nothing left to boast about. But Archie Thomson, who has lived in Renton all his days and knows his history and his people, is having none of it.

'We know we are the capital of Scotland, whatever that imposter over in the east has to say about it,' he insists when we meet. We had been getting the message from the moment we stepped off the train. Renton station building is now the Robert the Bruce Heritage Centre, run by Archie's brother, Duncan. The Bruce flew his hawks and hunted across these lands, moored his great oak boat in these waters and, when all his fighting was done, lived and died here. Even earlier, says Archie, the northwesterly march of the Roman Empire was halted when its foot soldiers stood atop Dumbarton Rock and surveyed the Vale of Leven below. 'They came, they saw, they retreated,' was how the early television historian, Dr Ian Grimble, put it half a century ago.

You quickly get the message that Renton folk see themselves as the real aristocracy of the Vale. It was here, in Dalquhurn House, that the novelist and naval surgeon Tobias Smollett was born. A fine stone column to his memory, erected by his cousin soon after he died, in Italy in 1771, aged just 50, stands in Renton's Main Street to this day.

But the chimneys of the great bleaching and printing works that gave this place its wealth, its plentiful skilled jobs and its sense of industrial purpose from the late eighteenth century for the best part of the next two hundred years are all long gone. Like Neilston, textiles made Renton.

'This was red Clydeside before communism was even invented,' says Archie. He isn't just talking about industrial militancy, though Renton was sometimes known as Little Moscow and this part of West Dumbartonshire still elects a Scottish Socialist Party councillor. He means Turkey Red, the distinctive dye for which the cloth dyeing and printing works on the Leven became famous, exporting most of what they produced to India, to China and the rest of Asia and to South America. This latterly was home to UTR, the United Turkey Red Company Ltd, the dominant world producer of the cloth. Until, that is, Gandhi's promotion of cottage industry production at home turned boom to bust back in the Vale.

'Gandhi said: If they can do it in the Renton, we can do it

Renton

63

here. So that was that,' is Archie Thomson's characteristically blunt take on that part of local history. After the war, there was a second industrial renaissance. On the other side of the Leven, in the Strathleven industrial estate, companies specialising in newer technologies, mainly from America, were moving in. Burroughs, assembling adding machines; Wiseman's, making lenses; Westclox; and Polaroid. A footbridge across the river gave workers from Renton easier access to these new jobs. But the new factories' life spans proved much shorter than the producers of textiles and turkey red. When they, in turn, went into decline, Renton fell on really hard times.

Archie Thomson went on right-to-work marches. The jobless numbers kept on rising. Despite all the top-down priority treatment policies, locally things were going from bad to worse.

'We were living in modern-day slums, with underfloor heating that never worked and cockroaches crawling over our food,' he recalls. 'And then the suits would appear and buy us football strips. The system never budged a millimetre. Their attitude was get behind us or get out.' He was having his own battle with alcohol. So, as relations with the regional and district councils became more fractious, as the statistics got worse and resources were pulled, Archie decided to walk away.

'Community politics can be a very dirty place,' he explains. In parts, Renton was looking increasingly derelict. Bereft. Eventually, when others came and asked him to come back and help stop the rot, he said, 'I'll only do it if we're taking these resources into community ownership.' It was the beginning of the 1990s. And the generic vehicle for doing just that was at hand in the shape of community housing associations. A steering group was established, feasibility studies completed and a ballot of tenants held. In 1993 Cordale Housing Association was formed. Part of its explicit promise from the start was: 'We won't build a better standard of housing for people to enjoy their poverty in.' It seems the entrepreneurial instinct to go beyond simply being a good social landlord was there from the start.

The council's response to Renton's decline had been to try and sell sites to private developers and change the names of local council housing schemes – Cordale became Kirkland – in the belief that that might alter the social mix and change the negative way tenants viewed themselves. From the start, the new housing association wanted to rebuild the community's resilience as well as construct trim semis. So one of its first acts was to bring back the old scheme names and adopt Cordale as its own identity.

The housing association's achievements since then are striking. The new Cordale estate, running down from Main Street to the banks of the Leven, is a pleasant community of well-maintained, mixed-tenure homes. Other transferred housing stock, in Back Street, on the other side of the village, has been transformed and is in high demand. There is, we are told, a 17-year waiting list there. The first phase of an ambitious plan to redevelop the former Dalquhurn estate, where Smollett was born, is complete. So far 129 houses have been built on the 30 acre site, after some of the heavily contaminated industrial land had been treated. Another 150 units are still on the drawing board.

But Cordale's pride and joy, as far as housing is concerned, is the building opened in 2009 locals call the Renton Hilton. Waterside View, right on Main Street but integrated with the other new housing around it, is a 40 apartment, extra care housing development, that encourages as much independent living as possible for some of the town's older residents. It's a bright and airy place. We were even invited back by some residents, sunning themselves in the garden. Come on Saturday evening, they told us, for our nightclub session! This is the place where, for instance, Sir Alex Ferguson, whose father came from Renton, has personally donated the trophy for the women's annual dominoes competition.

In all, so far, Cordale has provided more than 500 new and refurbished homes, around half the village's entire stock, predominantly for local people. But it's gone further than that. In the early years of the new millennium Archie Thomson, as chair of its management board, and Stephen Gibson, Cordale's director, decided they had to do something more radical than just building houses. There had been a eureka moment in late 2002 when, with local shops closing and council planners opting to focus retail activity four miles down the Vale in Alexandria, the pair had realised they could do some non-housing development on a commercial basis and recycle the proceeds into further regeneration of central Renton.

Cordale formed a trading subsidiary, secured funding support from the Clydesdale Bank, bought a site on Main Street from the council, demolished the existing dilapidated shops and built a modern 3000 sq.ft. retail unit. When it opened in 2004 it was leased to an Asian shopkeeper. It proved such a commercial success for him that he bought it outright two years later. It is now a busy Scotmid supermarket and post office. That and a fee-free ATM at the door reintroduced basic banking services to the village for the first time in three decades.

Some of the proceeds from the store deal were then used to redevelop a site directly opposite as a new Integrated Healthy Living Centre, providing space for two GP practices, ancillary services, such as podiatry and neurological clinics, and a full-time pharmacy. The centre, which opened in 2006, was a Scottish first for a housing association. 'Profit's not a bad word,' Archie insists. 'It's all about what you use that profit for.' The following three years were taken up with raising the funding to build the Renton Hilton, that exemplary community care complex for older citizens. Since it opened there's even been a discussion about Cordale's commercial arm building a new primary school campus in the village that would begin to break down the denominational divide in education.

Aware that their ambitions for the housing association were stretching conventional wisdom on who should be doing what, Archie Thomson had already been working with others to open up a second front in how to best tackle Renton's multiple disadvantages. In 1996, the council had opened an over 50s centre in the village. It had three badminton courts and what Archie describes as 'a soup kitchen' in the corner.

'I didn't know two people over the age of fifty in Renton who played badminton,' he recalls. By 2000, with help from local volunteers, it had been turned into a social inclusion centre, with a lively cafe, meeting rooms and space rented out to Job Centre Plus. Four years later SIPs were giving way to community planning partnerships but local community activists like Archie saw it as just a rebranding of the familiar top-down approach. They didn't play ball. They wanted an initiative the community itself could control.

Archie, who was aware of the emergence of development trusts as one way of delivering that, saw an opportunity to take over the centre and enhance the regeneration work already underway at Cordale Housing Association. So, in 2004, Renton Community Development Trust was launched and, with a 99-year lease from the council, the renamed Carman Centre, with ambitions to become a full-blown social enterprise, now became its base. At first the Trust and the centre maintained their separate identities. But, in 2009, they merged.

The aim from the start was to make the trust less dependent on grant funding and more of a revenue earner in its own right. That way a more sustainable future beckoned. Today the Carman Centre is a bustling community hub, where, as we talked, the first customers of the day were already drifting in. It is also home to a learning and training subsidiary, a popular community restaurant and contract catering business, a community care provider and, most recently, a grounds maintenance business. It also holds what's left of Renton public library's stock and has even managed to publish three books on local historical themes.

There are a number of synergies with how Cordale Housing Association operates. Carman Catering runs the restaurant in Waterside View. Carman Care provides support services there too, as well as a service to older residents in their own homes in the rest of Renton. In 2008 there was a further retreat from top-down provision of community assets in Renton. The council decided to close the local community education centre. But the community had other ideas. Shades of Twechar, the Trust was eventually given the building for nothing. After refurbishment it opened again last year as the Ma Centre, home to a variety of youth activities and to three businesses – a dance school, a photography studio and a boxing club.

Outside, they unveiled a statue of a bull, a tribute to five Renton men who fought fascism in Spain during the Civil War. Between them Cordale Housing Association and the Trust/Carman Centre are now the biggest employers in Renton. Cordale controls over half the entire housing stock. It is, on any measure, a remarkable transformation. It's a model of community regeneration that has since been copied elsewhere. We could have stayed longer and learned more. But our next leg of our journey was beckoning.

(Since we visited Renton, following a complaint from a member of staff, Archie Thomson has been removed from his role as chair of the board of Cordale Housing Association, while Stephen Gibson has been put on extended leave. The investigation into the complaint is ongoing. Archie Thomson retains his role at Renton Community Development Trust.)

FROM Renton we were heading for Comrie in rural west Perthshire. An advance exploration of the public transport options had shown it would take us four, even five, hours, by a combination of trains and buses, just to get there, leaving little time to do justice to our next story. So once more Carol stepped into the breach, picking us up from the Carman Centre. She grabbed some sandwiches, fruit and water from the supermarket next door while we said our goodbyes to Archie and his team. We ate while she drove us up Loch Lomondside to Crianlarich, then east on the A85, through Lochearnhead and St Fillans, to our destination. The fine weather since Dunbar was still with us along that ninety-minute drive. With cloudless skies and the temperature rising into the high twenties, the lochs and glens along our route had taken on an almost tropical magnificence.

This leg of our journey was taking us to a very different Scotland. Comrie, where three rivers – the Earn, Ruchill and Lednock – meet, appears, on first acquaintance, solid and prosperous. An attractive rural setting, especially popular with the retired perhaps? Reached by Agricola, and with some roots in weaving it is certainly not a place troubled by Renton's long history of industrial decline and social distress. However a few months after our visit, after heavy late August rains, the Water of Ruchill burst its banks and parts of the settlement suffered severe flooding, for the fourth time since 1993.

Some people call this village, which sits astride the highland fault line, the shaky toun. But there's nothing fragile about Comrie's community spirit. There may only be 2000 people on its electoral roll, but Comrie boasts around fifty active community groups. By the 1990s, its population was steadily ageing. The local primary school roll was falling. But in the past ten years, with an influx of younger residents, that roll's on the up again. It had reached 127 when we were there. With the rail connection at Dunblane just 22 miles away, some of Comrie's newer residents even commute to Edinburgh and Glasgow, we were told. But others are finding new ways of making their living in the local area.

This change in Comrie's demographic profile led to the people of the village having a big conversation of their own about what they wanted their village to be like in the future and what actions the community could take for itself to turn these ambitions into reality. Comrie was an early adopter of the development trust model.

Way back in March 2005, a group of local residents invited the sustainability officer from one of the real pioneers, the development Trust on the Orkney island of Westray, to come to Perthshire and help inspire their own thinking. Forty people turned up. By October that year, some 200 were involved in drawing up plans for a Trust of their own. Comrie Development Trust was formally launched the following July during a Comrie Alive festival that attracted a quarter of the entire village to a weekend of events.

'And today we have more than 700 members,' says Cathy Tilbrook proudly, 'that makes us one of the best represented development trusts anywhere in the UK'. Cathy was CDT's first chair. Working closely with the whole community –

individuals, groups and businesses – has always been a core principle for those who launched this trust. That way, they argue, they can capture and build community passion, enthusiasm, ideas and skills. Like many trusts, a core part of Comrie's original motivation was what could be done locally to meet the challenge of climate change. In its first three years, Comrie Carbon Challenge carried out a street-by-street energy audit and insulaton programme and a series of zero waste fortnight campaigns. A second three-year programme is now underway, including plans for a two-day youth climate conference.

From the start, the new trust was also determined to become financially self-sustaining. Members had their eyes on a redundant local asset that could help realise their dreams. While other communities pursue buy-ins to commercial renewable energy developments, CDT had in its sights on Cultybraggan, a defunct World War II POW camp, lying a mile and a half out of the village, complete with its 1990 addition, a large underground bunker capable of withstanding a nuclear attack.

'The camp is absolutely key to what happens next for Comrie,' says current Trust chair David McCall.

The Ministry of Defence had been indicating since 2004 it would put Cultybraggan Camp on the market. Unlike Ninian Stuart in Fife and his thousand huts campaign, the fledgling Trust in Comrie wasn't primarily driven by the opportunity to acquire nearly a hundred Nissen huts, some of them A and B-listed historic monuments, let alone take ownership of a former regional seat of government in Scotland, designed to run the country after a nuclear war. What attracted the Trust was getting control of 96 acres of Perthshire. On its doorstep. To be revived as 'a model of sustainable development for rural communities across Scotland.' Using the Land Reform (Scotland) Act 2003, CDT registered its community interest in buying Cultybraggan Camp. In May 2007, in a public ballot, the people of Comrie overwhelmingly endorsed that decision. A turnout of 72 per cent produced a 97 per cent majority in favour of the deal going ahead. By September 2007, the Trust had the keys to the camp. The price was £350,000, with the main loan funding coming from the Tudor Trust, later refinanced by longer-term loan finance from Triodos Bank.

The nuclear bunker alone had cost a reported £30m to build and was obsolete almost as soon as it was completed. Now that Comrie had ownership of Cultybraggan Camp, or Camp 21 as it was known in its POW days, the next big challenge was to put the site to productive and profitable community use. In January 2008 a Big Design day, to gather ideas and inspiration from the community for how the camp might be transformed, attracted some 400 participants. Master plans for Cultybraggan Camp, dividing the site into quadrants for everything from sporting facilities to an eco hub and space for new local enterprises, were then drawn up. Towards the end of 2008 the Trust produced its detailed plans for a sustainable future for Comrie right through to 2014. The challenge statement in that plan is a fine encapsulation of its mission:

> We need to look at how we become more self-sufficient; how we move about; how we provide energy and food; how we provide workshop space for people who can fix things; how we entertain ourselves and look after each other. In other words, how we build a resilient community.

Having talked with Cathy and David in the Trust's office in the middle of Comrie we then went, with vice-chair Peter Jones and board member Emma Margrett, to see Cultybraggan Camp for ourselves. In the food quadrant forty local families are now growing more of their own food in the allotments. The community orchard was planted in March 2011. There are hens and a commercial shiitake mushroom business and a polytunnel for Comrie in Colour, the group that masterminds the village's floral displays. The mess block, the most modern structure on the site, has been rented to Wilde Thyme, an award-winning event catering and party planning business. So far 14 businesses have taken space at the camp, in some of the other refurbished huts. In total they employ the equivalent of 44 full-time staff so far.

The Trust had to invest in the site initially to improve drainage, sewerage, water and power supplies. It has also invested in a biomass boiler-fired district heating system. Planning permission has been granted for the restoration of grass pitches and the creation of other facilities in the sports quadrant. And for the A-listed core of the camp, it's jail building, plans are being pursued to fund and build a futures centre, including a small museum/heritage centre, a cafe and high quality space that could host meetings and small conferences and provide a permanent base for the Trust and its mission to reduce Comrie's carbon footprint.

Even that bunker, having seen off any nuclear or biological apocalypse, could soon have a new lease of commercial life. As a secure data storage vault. In January 2012 GCI Com, a Lincoln-based data networking group, entered into a joint venture deal with the Trust to create a new data centre within the bunker. Under the terms of the deal, CDT would get a capital receipt and a share of annual profits. In the early years, the money would be reinvested in the data centre. But in the longer term, once the Trust's borrowings have been redeemed, revenues would be used to benefit the community. Crucially, since the data centre will require high speed broadband to operate, the benefits of that will become available to the entire Comrie community. Big city broadband speeds available in this corner of rural Perthshire. What might that do for this local economy?

When Camp 21 housed some of its most fervent Nazi prisoners, dark deeds followed. Three inmates were murdered there. Two because they were suspected of being British spies. A third because he was not one of them. Five of those suspected of killing Wolfgang Rosterg were found guilty after trial in London and hanged at Pentonville, the largest multiple execution carried out in twentieth century Britain.

But as the 2010 history of the camp, written by the Cultybraggan Camp Local History Group for the Trust shows, there have been acts of reconciliation too. Another prisoner, Heinrich Steinmeyer, was so impressed by the fair treatment he received from his captors he vowed publicly in 2009 to leave his entire estate to the elderly people of Comrie when he dies. However improbable it may seem, both in the plans its current owners have for it and in Herr Steinmeyer's remarkable gesture, the legacy of Cultybraggan Camp for its host village is one that just keeps on giving.

We caught an early evening bus out of Comrie, headed for Perth. The Stagecoach service had been held up by a traffic accident on its way from St Fillans and the driver was anxious to make up for lost time. The journey east on the A85, through Crieff, took us past Ochtertyre, the country estate of Sir Brian Souter, co-founder with his sister Ann Gloag, of the Stagecoach transport group. The grand Georgian mansion looked down on us across the sunlit waters of Loch Monzievaird. Frivolously we speculated on whether its owner might be at a window as we passed, checking out the punctuality of his 15A service.

On the way into Perth, Ewan had used his phone to identify another bus service that might take us on to Dundee. Run by a bus operator neither of us had ever heard of, improbably this one started in Fort William and ended in Brechin! We dashed round the corner into South Street to see if it turned up. The scheduled pick-up time came and went. We wanted to get to Dundee in time to see Tiril's degree show at Duncan of Jordanstone, Dundee University's renowned college of art and design, before it closed for the night. So we decided on a second dash to Perth's main bus station where we soon caught a Citylink service. Tiril is Ewan's wife Merlin's sister.

This bus deposited us in the City of Jute in time to check in to a local Travelodge and get up to the college to see her work. But it was turning into a very long day. A steam train was making its majestic way south across the Tay Bridge, as we walked back down the Perth Road to the Nethergate, in search of somewhere to eat. The kitchen in one of our favourite pubs, the Phoenix Bar, was closed, so we went elsewhere When we went back for a pint the landlord asked us where we'd eaten. 'Oh that one's owned by a Glasgow gangster who drives around here in a big Bentley,' he confided. We were careful not to be overheard rating the food.

From an Inspiring Oasis in the City of Jute to our search for Transitions in Moray

IN THE morning we grabbed a bacon roll and some orange juice from a local sandwich bar and decided to take a taxi up to the Hilltown, where our eleventh – and oldest – community enterprise is based. Dundee International Women's Centre was established in 1969. Back then it was an urban aid project, aimed specifically at supporting Asian women who had come to Dundee because of the city's jute mills.

'Our oldest member,' notes Gwendoline Telford, DIWC's Culture and Diversity team leader, 'came here by car from the Punjab. And when she got here, the prevailing local fashion was mini-skirts and go-go boots. She must have thought she had landed on the moon.'

For most of its existence the centre was housed in a cramped flat in a tenement block in Lyon Street. Nowadays it occupies a single-storey industrial unit, further up the hill, on the site of one of those jute mills, nestling unobtrusively between a furniture factory and a wholesale carpet warehouse. The shed-like exterior does nothing to prepare the first-time visitor for the dynamic and welcoming initiative

Dundee

77

housed beyond that orange-painted front door. On the wall in the reception area is a map of the world, indicating the growing range of countries from which DIWC's members are drawn. There were 473 of them in the past year, each paying a £3 annual membership fee. Over the past five years the centre has worked with 1235 different women. Their ethnic origins span the globe. South Asia, at 36 per cent, still accounts for the largest group. Eastern Europe now contributes 20 per cent. East Asia 12 per cent. With smaller percentages from the Middle East, North and Southern Africa and North and South America.

The centre offers them a rich diversity of experiences and support. From confidence building classes in sewing, arts and crafts and cooking, through English conversation classes and a UK citizenship study group, to more formal qualifications in English, computing and childcare. There are social groups for young women (from 12 to 21), for mothers and toddlers, and for the over 50s. The average age in the latter group is currently seventy! There's information and advice, including translation services (the staff speak nine languages); practical support with form-filling and the like; and advocacy on everything from benefits to domestic abuse, from housing to employment rights.

'We aim to provide a holistic service,' says Gwendoline, who joined originally as a volunteer a decade ago, when the centre was still in its bustling flat down the hill. Many who came in the seventies, she explains, were from patriarchal families where women were not encouraged to engage with the outside world, let alone go out to work. The big challenge was to provide them with an environment where they felt comfortable. A safe space where they could begin to find their feet in an unfamiliar culture. Learn how to register their kids for school. Use the post office. Or access GP and hospital services. The services provided evolved with time to include English classes, IT and social groups to support women who were isolated. In-house child care was also provided to ensure women with young children could engage.

'In Lyon Street we had to bring in child care workers,' she continues. 'Then we thought: Why don't we train the women we work with to do that? We didn't realise we were embarking on a social enterprise. But soon we started to understand that's what it was. We're very passionate about social enterprise now.'

Gwendoline's other passion is for putting together funding applications. That matters because, to function effectively, DIWC is still heavily dependent on grant funding from a range of public bodies and charities. Just over 84 per cent of the centre's income in 2011/12 came from donations and grants. However, it is making steady progress in growing two money-making social enterprises of its own – the evolution of that childcare initiative, now called Rise & Shine Childcare and Creche, and the Wooden Spoon Catering Co.

The story of how Wooden Spoon came to be five years ago is remarkable. Some of the women who came to the centre had been involved for some time in cookery classes. They had brought with them their own special recipes, notably curries. Curries cooked in the traditional way, slowly for up to five hours. To generate some income, DIWC had been renting out one of its rooms to companies for training. Some users asked if they could provide lunch too. So the group involved in the cookery class began to provide some buffet food. Curry quickly became the speciality of choice. Then, with the centre's own activities growing, space was at a premium and the room lets had to stop. But companies continued to use the buffet service. The idea of a full-blown catering business began to germinate. It was decided, despite the confines of the centre's domestic-scale kitchen, to test the market. For the Friday of the three-day Camperdown Flower and Food Festival 2008, the centre cooked 400 litres of curry to sell to festival goers.

'Everyone mucked in,' recalls Gwendoline. 'But we knew we were onto something. You can't get curry like this anywhere.' Sadly that Friday the site at Camperdown flooded. The centre needed a plan B. So a telesales campaign to everyone they could think of swung into action. Almost all the curry was shifted. DIWC's Friday Night Curry Night was born. Rapidly some ninety workplaces in the city were taking weekly deliveries.

Enter the Wooden Spoon Catering Co. Dundee has long been known as the city of jute, jam and journalism. But, in the digital age, print journalism is struggling to survive. Even the oldest comic produced on Tayside, D C Thomson's *Dandy* faces closure. However, thanks to DIWC, there's now a fourth J. In the spring of 2011, at a civic dinner welcoming the launch of the Wooden Spoon Catering Co website a few months earlier, the theme of the evening was Jute, Jam and Jalfrezi! One of the doyens of Glasgow's commercial curry scene, Charan Gill, was there to praise the quality of the DIWC women's cooking. There too was Paul Grant, who has kept the area's jam making tradition alive through the Mackays brand, produced in nearby Carnoustie.

Wooden Spoon has been an independent company since May 2010, albeit one 100 per cent owned by DIWC. It moved out of the centre, again for space reasons, to the cafe in the council-owned Olympia swimming pool complex on the waterfront. But, with the old Olympia due to close at the end of 2012, it is now embarking on the next stage of its development. It already sells its food online. And has secured a £113,000 grant, from the Scottish government's Social Enterprise Growth Fund, to build and equip an industrial scale kitchen. When we were there, it had located shop-front premises in Castle Street to open a retail deli. Staff increased from 7 to 16 in 2011/12 and a dedicated training programme has been put in place to encourage more members to develop their catering skills and find work, either within the expanding Wooden Spoon or elsewhere. If this social enterprise can keep its promise to produce food of the same exceptional quality, the prospects of it delivering the revenue stream DIWC wants to balance its need for grant funding the future look very bright.

One of the conditions of much of its funding is that the centre focuses on serving the Hilltown and Stobswell areas of the city. However women from all over Dundee – and indeed the world – access a wide range of educational and support services.

On our brief acquaintance this is a very special place. You feel uplifted and inspired just to have been there. Remarkably, there's nothing quite like it anywhere else in Scotland. The nearest parallel outside Scotland, Gwendoline tells us, is the First Steps Women's Centre serving Dungannon and South Tyrone. But its focus is on healing Northern Ireland's sectarian divide. Given the growing demand for its holistic range of services, DIWC may eventually have to move to bigger premises, perhaps a greener place in Dundee. Sharing a car park with massive articulated trailers, moving furniture, isn't easy. But this legacy of the city's jute heritage is one anonymous industrial shed with a heart of gold.

As we said our goodbyes the late morning sun was pushing temperatures even higher. We had a little time to spare before our train north. So we decided to walk back down to the station, stirring memories of past walks after Morton games at Dens Park or Tannadice. Ewan had even had a brief teenage flirtation with Dundee United before he joined his father, Alf, and younger brother, Jamie, as a long-suffering Morton fan.

The journey to Aberdeen passed without incident. There we bought some food-to-go in the concourse and boarded an Inverness-bound train that would take us to our next destination, Forres. On this service the air-conditioning had packed in. The carriage promised to be sweltering. As our train passed under Union Street and skirted Castle Terrace Gardens, then still embroiled in controversy over whether they should be preserved or transformed into something more twenty first century, the grass was thick with lunchtime sun worshippers. At Dyce a number of offshore workers, heading home, took up any available seats. Welcome to the Speyside-bound sauna! The extensive housing developments around Inverurie reminded us of Neilston. By Keith we were looking out on the Glentauchers Distillery and the Chivas bond. Strange to think that UDV mothballed Glentauchers in 1985 before selling it to Allied in 1989. And that Diageo, the current incarnation of UDV, is now building new distillery capacity in the area and looking to expand production at some of the other Speyside distilleries it still owns. When it comes to the Scotch whisky industry, market forecasting appears to be a far from perfect science.

IT WAS a relief to step out of our Scotrail sauna at Forres, to be greeted by our next host, Carin Schwartz. We had come to talk about the transition town movement, something that originated in the United Kingdom in the historic market town of Totnes, at the head of the Dart estuary, in Devon. Transition towns – which don't, as it happens, have to be towns – try to take into their own hands their community's response to peak oil and climate change. They are trying to design their own way through the challenges.

'We can't just wait for governments and local authorities to do things for us. We need to start doing something for ourselves,' typifies the sentiments of those drawn to the transition town movement. One of its prime movers was Rob Hopkins, with ideas he developed when a teacher of permaculture at a further education college in Kinsale in the Irish Republic. Totnes became his home town. Both Kinsale and Totnes embraced the challenge. And now there are literally thousands of communities worldwide involved and more than 300 in the UK. In Scotland, apart from Forres, they range from Portobello and Biggar, to Moffat and the North Howe in

Forres

Fife. For those who don't know Fife well that's the communities of Collessie, Letham and Giffordtown, just east of Ninian Stuart at Falkland. There's another covering the Black Isle.

The UK pioneer. Totnes, is a prosperous place with a reputation for welcoming those seeking an alternative life style. Look at its Wikipedia entry and you find words like 'funky' and 'new age' used to describe it. Forres too, despite its struggling high street – there's a Tesco on the western edge of town – exudes an air of quiet prosperity. Over twenty years its volunteer Forres in Bloom group has scooped too many awards to list individually here, culminating in the Entente Florale Europe gold award in 2009. And, of course, it has its alternative hinterland, at the Findhorn Foundation, with its spiritual community, ecovillage and international centre for holistic education, sitting ten minutes drive away north, across the A96 trunk road.

Swedish-born Carin first came to the area in 2005 to take a course at Findhorn. She had spent almost thirty years as an international banker, working in Stockholm, New York, Berlin and London. She was entranced by what she found in this part of Moray. And so disillusioned with where the world of big money was heading, she decided to quit banking and make the area home. In 2008 she was instrumental in creating Transition Town Forres. From the station she drove us to TTF's community garden, for late afternoon tea and some home baking. Joining us were two other TTF directors. Donald Rodgie, from Milngavie, but with family roots in Forres, spent most of his career in London as a stockbroker. Now he builds inventive polytunnels and grows more of his own food. He's contemplating getting involved in a social enterprise too.

Sandra Maclennan was head teacher of a local primary school, Applegrove, until she retired. Now she's busier than ever, with TTF and as chair of Forres in Bloom. Since our visit, Forres has been awarded yet another Gold Medal in the prestigious RHS Britain in Bloom Champion of Champions category.

We had tea in the Bogton community garden, in front of a log cabin. It is all that's left of a short-lived commercial landscaping business. The land where we sat is common good land. But TTF had a year-long struggle with officialdom to get its lease on this land.

'I had asked for land for allotments from Moray Council,' Carin explains. 'But they strung us along. Then they called us up and told us we couldn't have allotments, because of the provisions of an act of 1884.' TTF had funding from the Climate Challenge Fun to pay for any lease. But time was running out on that offer. It became clear the council's problem was that, if allotments were established, they might never be able to get the holders off the site again.

'What if we make it a community garden?' Carin suggested. They got their eleven-year lease and the keys two weeks later, just before the promised funding lapsed. The lease has now been extended to thirty years. Instead of individual allotments, TTF decided to create twelve circular pods, each divided into four plots. In all some seventy adults are now actively involved in growing things, helped by nearly as many children. The accent is on interaction and skill sharing, rather than competitive show-based horticulture. Permaculture principles are encouraged but not compulsory. There is, however, a ban on using chemicals, either as fertilizers or pesticides. Carin's pride and joy is the extensive wormery. And there's a mountain of leaf mould on the way now thanks to cooperation with Moray Council each autumn when the many trees around town shed their foliage. The terms of the lease also allows three beehives and up to thirty chickens.

The people involved in TTF are a diverse lot. Not as varied as the members of the Dundee International Women's Centre perhaps. But there are some retired and redundant RAF personnel, from what was until recently RAF Kinloss nearby, who decided to stay on in the area. We met one, happily pushing his wheelbarrow. And there are people from France, Brazil, Portugal and Germany. For the first two years, they ran monthly farmers' markets in the community garden car park. TTF have also distributed a local food guide. They've had more than 500 people attend the market on occasions. But that venture has stalled somewhat. Recession hasn't helped. And there's increasing competition. Elgin has started offering free pitches for its farmers' market, through a BID (business improvement district) initiative.

'We will start up again,' say Carin. 'We might even try to do it weekly and offer discounts if stallholders agree to come regularly. But it all depends on funding.' Their plans for the log cabin or pavilion, as they call it, is to turn it into a real community hub. An environmental education and healthy living centre, where another part of the skill sharing agenda will be a From Pod to Plate programme. That means teaching people, who are learning to grow things, how to make the most cost-effective use of their produce to feed their families with soups, bakes, sauces and even leftovers. A creative cuisine for hard times.

TTF has installed a biomass pellet boiler in the pavilion both as a cost-effective source of heating and as a practical demonstration of alternative energy sources. The snag is that the pavilion, in planning terms, is still classified as an agricultural building. Until they get a change of use from the authorities and can raise the funding to complete the cabin's conversion, it remains a work in progress. For Forres there's still a long way to go before they can think of launching initiatives on water usage, transport, waste or the introduction of a local currency – the kind of things some of the pioneer transition towns have already shown can be done.

Totnes has its Totnes pound. Kinsale has its energy descent action plan. Back in October 2009, Transition Town Forres held a public event in the local Ramnee Hotel, boldly themed Visioning Forres in 2025. That produced an ambitious and detailed step-by-step blueprint of how to get there. But the partner organisation present that evening, Transition Scotland Support, came to an end in March 2011 when its funding was withdrawn. If transition town initiatives across Scotland are to realise all their dreams, there needs to be much more consistent backing from public bodies at all levels for this kind of initiative.

We've noted the loss of RAF Kinloss earlier. In July the base was officially handed over to an arm of the British Army, 39 Regiment (Air Support). That will lessen the impact of the loss of RAF Kinloss on the area. But there is still concern about the economic damage that could follow. So, in September 2011, with funding from Highlands and Islands LEADER a new initiative, Forres Area Community Trust (FACT) was launched, charged with the regeneration of the greater

87

Forres area, effectively the catchment area of the local secondary school, Forres Academy. It has the money to employ two full-time equivalent development officers. TTF had a project manager at one point. But the funding for that only lasted a year. Carin, as well as being the founder and a director of TTF, is now also a member of the FACT board.

We wish the volunteers of the transition town initiative in Forres well. It was good to see that an initiative that involves a former international banker and a one-time City of London stockbroker, benefits from funds raised at musical evenings with the theme: You Can't Eat Money. It's a take on a nineteenth century Cree Indian warning. 'Only when the last tree has died, and the last river has been poisoned, and the last fish has been caught, will we realise that we cannot eat money.'

But money is needed for communities to realise their dreams. And without more tangible support, it seems to us that TTF may struggle, now that FACT is up and running, to do everything it wants to do on the timetable it has set itself. After a tour of the town and a quick run out to Findhorn to see her new home, nearing completion on the edge of the existing community, Carin took us back to the railway station for the last short leg of our day's journey, to Inverness. We checked in at the Ramada Encore in Academy Street and went off to the music pub, Hootananny, in Church Street, for a pint and some welcome food.

A Morning on the Kyle Line
then over the Bridge to Sleat

ANOTHER quick breakfast, this time in Inverness station, and we boarded the nine o'clock train, bound for Kyle of Lochalsh. That two-and-a-half hour journey – especially when undertaken on another gloriously sunny morning, as we were – is one of life's joys. Michael Palin's done it for his great railway journeys of the world. Many years before, Alf and Carol had even experienced it with live musical accompaniment. On an old-fashioned train with corridors and compartments for six, with members of the Scottish Chamber Orchestra on board. Along the way players moved from compartment to compartment, in twos and threes, playing short pieces for passengers. Chugging into Attadale station to a harp and flute duet is hard to beat.

Back then, at Kyle, all aboard retired to the local hotel and, over lunch, the SCO musicians came together and put on an impromptu concert. This morning our twenty first century Scotrail carriage was busy with tourists, walkers and rough terrain cyclists, many to be deposited at one of the thirteen stops (some by request only) along the way. While the landscapes we were passing through were, as ever, a rich feast for the eye, travel in this part of Scotland can be challenging. A few months earlier there had been a major rockfall on the A890 at Stromeferry, leaving locals with a 140 mile detour, via Inverness, to get to school or work. Eventually the authorities resorted to allowing cars to drive along a short section of the rail line, coupled with the temporary reintroduction of an old ferry service across Loch Carron, until the blockage was eventually cleared.

When we reached Kyle, we had a short dash with our bags round to the old slipway to pick up a bus that would take us over the Skye Bridge and, after a small detour into Kyleakin, on to Broadford. Our driver confirmed that, from there, we could soon get a bus back down to South Skye and our next destination, Armadale, on the Sleat Peninsula. But when we got to Broadford, the promised bus from Portree never arrived. It was listed on the shelter timetable. Some French hikers were waiting for it too. But, as we stood there in the baking noon sun, it gradually dawned on us all it wasn't coming. We learned later that it only runs when the schools are on holiday. There wouldn't be one at this time of day until July! But there would be a bus to Sleat. If we waited another ninety minutes for it.

We spent the time having a lunch of toasted sandwiches and salad at the cafe across the road. Then we chatted to Janet, a native of Sleat despite her accent, who had spent most of her life working in the health service in England, but had come home to retire. She was in Broadford to stock up on groceries. When the bus finally came she and Jimmy, the driver, treated us to a rich, running commentary on life in this part of Skye. The resident population of the island as a whole is just under 10,000. But in summer it swells fourfold. There are around 900 people resident in Sleat, up a hundred or so in less than a decade. Thanks to the year-round CalMac car ferry service between Mallaig and Armadale, and the presence of the Clan Donald centre and the Gaelic College, Sabhal Mor Ostaig, Sleat gets more than its pro-rata share of the island's abundant visitors. This is a vibrant part of the West Highlands. A sustainable growth point, if only support structures are in place to help it go on thriving.

We had come to meet Angus Robertson, manager of Sleat Community Trust. The Trust was incorporated back in 2004. It was brought into being as one community's response to a proposed major wind farm development on its doorstep. One of the major UK utilities, npower, was planning to put turbines on a local estate, a forerunner of both Fintry and Neilston. The original *raison d'être* of this Trust was to see what local benefits could be won from the developer. But this wind farm project was stillborn. Grid connection charges and the overall costs of the installation proved insurmountable.

So the infant Trust had to find other challenges. A big one arrived the following year when the proprietor of the only local filling station, at the ferry terminal road head in Armadale, retired. The business was put on the market. Two years later it still hadn't sold. So in 2007, after consulting the community, the Trust bought the filling station and shop and a bungalow on the site. There's not much money to be made out of selling petrol from a single site. But this site is a vital link on a major tourist route and a lifeline for a remote community. So Sleat Community Trading's investment, done with help from the Big Lottery, was a statement of clear intent.

Angus and his small team use the house as their office. The shop at the filling station, which now incorporates the local post office and a visitor information centre, is being extended to allow for more retail space and a small office with internet connection for local and visitor use. And there's a garage and MOT centre on the site, leased to a local mechanic. The Trust administers on behalf of Highland Council a subsidised taxi service for local people. Some compensation for the poor local bus service. 'It's not for going to the pub,' says Angus. The Trust also publishes *An Sleiteach*, the community's monthly newsletter.

Building up the Trust's trading and community engagement activities was followed by a much bigger leap forward. Towards the southern tip of Sleat lies the thousand-acre Tormore forest. It was a Forestry Commission Scotland asset. But the mature plantation was landlocked. Sea access was difficult. And local roads were judged inadequate to get felled timber out. So, in July 2011, after years of negotiations, persuading FCS they were fit and proper people to manage a large forest, and with help from a range of backers, including Highland Council, Highlands and Islands Enterprise and Triodos Bank, the Trust completed the purchase of the entire forest for £330,000. Now Tormore Community Forest.

Local buy-in to the deal is impressive. The Trust has 470 members, over 70 per cent of the local adult population. When it was sought, support for taking felled timber out of Tormore, on a controlled time and speed basis, by an upgraded road through Ardvasar, was overwhelming. In the first two years more than 20,000 tonnes of mainly Sitka will be dispatched, to chip board processing plants and to sawmills. This is the Sleat Trust's answer to long-term financial sustainability.

'We'll still need grant support for specific programmes,' says Angus. 'Raising core funding for running costs is never easy and indeed it's getting even harder now. But the big revenue earner will be the forest. We've got a felling plan for Tormore that could stretch out forty years.' This venture isn't just about harvesting the mature timber. There's a replanting programme. Enhanced forest management, including installing miles of new fencing. Opening up areas of the forest for mountain biking and nature trails. Even identifying areas for green burials.

Well before the Tormore deal was sealed, the Trust already had an active renewables subsidiary. It's been chipping bought-in logs and supplying the biomass boiler at the Gaelic college for some time. That business will now become an integral part of its development programme at Tormore. Since we were there the Trust has won £30,000 in the Santander Social Enterprise Awards towards building a covered facility for its wood fuel business.

Like many of the trusts we visited, Sleat Renewables has had money from the Climate Challenge Fund and has acquired equipment, including a rotovator, a log splitter, a shredder and a log trailer, available on free hire to local people to encourage more vegetable growing and more use of local heating fuel. Allotments are available at Armadale's community garden.

Despite the failure of the wind farm project that led to the

Trust's creation it has continued to explore the prospects of investing in a 900 kW community turbine on a roadside hill at the north end of the peninsula. Wind speeds have been monitored over an extended period. Despite investment of some tens of thousands of pounds in what Angus calls a 'long and weary' process, one major obstacle remains. The company that controls grid access, SSE, says it would be 2020 at the earliest before that would be possible. So the Trust is now exploring the economics of a community turbine that might provide embedded power to a large consumer within the Sleat community.

Other important collaborations locally are ongoing, notably on plans by the Clan Donald Lands Trust, which runs the Clan Donald centre and manages some 20,000 acres of the peninsula. It has opened an abattoir to process venison locally rather than send it to Dingwall. And has outline planning permission to build a brand new village at Kilbeg, near the college. 'If the funding can be raised, it would be the first new village in the Highlands for a hundred years,' says Angus.

With very little social housing currently available in Sleat, the Community Trust is a major consultee within the project. The masterplan, to be delivered over twenty years, would see 93 homes built, together with new student residences and teaching space for the college, an added conference facility, enterprise workshops, a residential care home, hotel accommodation, a retail outlet and cafe bar, sports facilities and public open spaces.

From what we saw and heard, Sleat is a thriving community with all the main players working in concert to build on what has already been achieved. A competition for a new strapline that captured the ethos of the Trust produced this winning entry. In Gaelic, *an-diugh, a-maireach, combla.* Today, tomorrow, together.

In 2011, the Community Trust was awarded the Queen's Award for Voluntary Service. That's a tribute to the efforts of its nine-strong board and staff of five, one part-time. Looking forward it's not without its challenges. Just before we arrived, for instance, Transport Scotland caused some alarm locally by suggesting the Armadale-Mallaig ferry link might no longer be regarded as 'absolutely essential'.

When we parted company with Angus, it had become so hot we bought a couple of mint ice lollies from Niall in the filling station shop and walked slowly up through Ardvasar to check in at our B&B. Our hosts at Homeleigh were Jan, originally from Australia and Peter, from Hampshire. When we told them what we were up to, Jan revealed their home had been the post office before they bought it. She had briefly been the sub-postmistress, before handing the business over to the Trust. Reluctantly, for family reasons, they had put the place up for sale and planned on moving to south-west Scotland. 'We've had forty nationalities staying with us,' she said. 'We've done some business fifty weeks in each year. In peak season we could let ten rooms, rather than the three we've got. We'll be sorry to go.'

Peter chipped in with a story of trying to phone the island when callers still had to be connected by operators. 'Get me Skye please,' he said. Only to hear the operator respond. 'Skye doesn't exist. It's just a dream place.'

95

Bound for a Whale of a Time on Eigg

AFTER a hearty breakfast at Homeleigh, our hosts offered to drive us down to the ferry terminal to catch the 8.50 sailing of the *Coruisk* to Mallaig. The previous evening we had treated ourselves to a leisurely meal at the Ardvasar Hotel. Afterwards we walked a couple of miles down the road past the entrance to Tormore Community Forest until, as we rounded a bend, in what felt like a tropical gloaming, we caught our first sight of our next destination. The unmistakable contours of the Island of Eigg.

In Mallaig we had time to send off a couple of postcards to Carol and to her sister Marianne in Brighton. This series is called Postcards from Scotland, after all. Next a short train journey from Mallaig to Arisaig, in the company of a group of excited youngsters, with their teachers, headed for a picnic on the beach. The walk from Arisaig station takes you across the railway line and down a path until you meet the main A830 road and the main part of the village beyond. Just before we got to the road we came upon a young stag, casually grazing a few yards away on a grass verge. He seemed quite unperturbed as we burst in on his breakfast. Having surveyed us with regal disdain, he moved off, jumped a wall into a field, looked round at us once more and was off.

We had originally planned to get back from Eigg in time to take the Friday evening sailing to Inverie and stay there for the night. But there wasn't a bed to be had in Knoydart that weekend. Someone was getting married. Taking a tent and sleeping bags with us all the way for the sake of one night had seemed onerous. Happily the parents of our next-door neighbour in Strathblane, Nikola, have a house in Arisaig and had offered to put us up. Neil and Eileen weren't going to be there until later in the day. So we left our bags round the back of their house and headed down to the harbour to collect our tickets and board Arisaig Marine's *Sheerwater*.

What a week of sun we had had. Its glorious rays had brought the tourists out. Our boat was busy. The crossing to Eigg felt like we were cruising the Greek islands. Or threading our way in to Saanich on Vancouver Island. The whole experience was enhanced by the determination of our skipper, Ronnie, to show us some wildlife before we stepped ashore. We expected to see seals and shearwaters and other sea birds. And did. But Ronnie knew there were Minke whales around. He was determined to track some of them down too. He did. With the shimmering peaks of Rum framing the far distance, how we oohed and aahed as their sleek forms broke surface, again and again. Finally, we arrived at the jetty in Galmisdale Bay and stepped ashore.

The redoubtable Maggie Fyffe was there, amidst a throng on the pier, to greet us. We repaired to the back terrace at An

Eigg

Laimhrig, the Isle of Eigg Heritage Trust's first building project and now the island's social hub, to talk. We were joined by Eddie Scott, another more recent Eigg resident, who was going to show us round its custom-built electric power system.

The story of how this Small Isles community won control of its own destiny by buying its island has been told before. The history of feudal abuse that, as the late John Lorne Campbell, enlightened owner of sister island Canna, once put it, saw Eigg and its people 'kicked around' by a succession of quixotic landowners who didn't share his enlightened approach is well documented. Eigg was bought in 1975 by Keith Schellenberg, a Yorkshire businessman and one-time Winter Olympian, married into an aristocratic family that owned Udny Castle in Aberdeenshire. He had bought his Small Isle from a man who claimed to be a retired naval commander, running a charity for deprived boys, later uncovered as a junior officer in the London Fire Brigade, exploiting the kids as slave labour. Schellenberg would then sell, twenty years later, to a bogus German fire artist who called himself Maruma, in hock to a Hong Kong businessman!

Maggie and her husband, Wes, came to Eigg in 1976, as part of Schellenberg's plans to repopulate the place with younger blood, including artists and crafts people.

'It was good for a few years,' she recalls. 'People were really welcoming and he had lots of good ideas, like building up a holiday business. But he was pretty eccentric and messed people about. And, if you fell out with him, you were on a really fine line.' The big issue was tenure. Most people were living in tied cottages. Some in appalling condition. And every attempt to secure leases from his estate on homes and workshops was rebuffed. Many people gave up and left. The Fyffes were lucky. They managed to get a croft. Others ended up living in caravans on crofts, just to get out of his control.

'His biggest fault was he wouldn't give anyone security,' says Maggie. 'It could all have been so different if he had just offered folk leases on their homes.' But Schellenberg had problems of his own. He and his wife had divorced in 1981. But she controlled a half share in Eigg and was becoming increasingly concerned about how he was managing their joint investment. There was increasing talk that he would be forced to sell. If he did, might the community of Eigg be able to mount a buy-out? The first attempt came in 1991, not from the islanders themselves, but from a group of four supporters. We both know two of them. Tom Forsyth who, until recently, lived in Scoraig. And Alastair McIntosh, whom we had encountered the previous Monday, outside GalGael in Govan. Alf had also met Liz Lyon in the 1970s, when she lived in Gartocharn. The fourth was Bob Harris.

Together, they formed the Isle of Eigg Trust, with the aim of raising money to buy Schellenberg out. To this day Maggie teases Alastair that they formed their Trust without telling anyone on the island. The islanders, many of them fearful and lacking the confidence to take on Schellenberg themselves, did back the initiative. But then their laird bought his ex-wife's interest out and took Eigg off the market. Without a willing seller, that Trust initiative was going nowhere.

'We wanted the leases sorted out. We wanted a community hall. And we wanted the paperwork sorted out so that Lochaber Housing Association could build five houses on Eigg for social needs,' says Maggie. 'It looked as if things might improve. But then it just went to hell.' Relations with the laird plummeted. He even tried to have a couple of families evicted. The island's retired doctor, the only one who felt free to speak out, told the BBC it was like 'living under enemy occupation'.

The shed in which Schellenberg's vintage Rolls Royce was stored mysteriously burned down. The only bright spots were that the crofters in Assynt had just succeeded in buying their land and the quartet who started the Eigg Trust had passed control of any future community buy-out on Eigg to its residents. So they started to do the groundwork.

But there was to be one more twist in the Eigg story before they got their chance. In March 1995 Schellenberg announced he'd sold Eigg to Marlin Eckhart who styled himself Maruma, for £1.5m. The new owner turned up just twice, that April and July, each time for a couple of days. Maggie and the other residents tried to engage him with the development plan they'd put together from the previous winter's series of discussions. He sounded enthusiastic but there was no follow-up. Instead he ordered the estate's indigenous herd of cattle to be sent to auction on the mainland. Staffing on the estate was pared back and then Maruma stopped paying the two who were left. A welter of faxes from the residents went unanswered. In 1996 land agents arrived, clearly preparing for another sale, this time with a guide price of £2m. The residents made it their business to tell any potential buyers who turned up that they would be doing so against the express wishes of the community.

But they did more. With help from Stornoway lawyer, Simon Fraser, an iconic figure in Scotland's community land movement, they set up Isle of Eigg Heritage Trust, with representation from the residents, Highland Council and the Scottish Wildlife Trust, with Fraser as its first independent chairman. And they launched their own public appeal for money to fund their buy-out. Helped by widespread publicity about their plight, notably a *Guardian* newspaper piece headlined Lairds of Misrule, promises of support from members of the public rolled in.

Public agencies that might have helped were wary. But eventually they had enough pledges to bid what they were told was the true market value, £1.2m. Even that bid would not have been possible had it not been for the support of one mystery woman living in the north of England who had never visited the island. Originally she pledged £500,000. Then, when a bid for support to the Heritage Lottery Fund failed because it insisted on control residing not with the residents but in some conservation body, her final contribution was worth £1m of the total. Maggie spoke to her many times during the sale process. But the Eigg residents' principal benefactor has always chosen anonymity and the community has always respected that. In the end just £17,000 of the purchase fund came from the public purse, from Highlands and Islands Enterprise. At first the Trust's offer to buy was rejected. But when, in 1997, it heard that Maruma had defaulted on a loan from his Hong Kong backer, where Eigg was the security, they saw their chance. After a week of tense negotiations and covert visits to lawyers in Edinburgh, they took ownership of their island.

After the celebrations, the big question, Maggie remembers vividly, 'was what are we going to do now?' They had done a lot of thinking and debating in the run up to the sale. Now they had to deliver. One immediate challenge was to sort out housing security. Residents were given the option to buy their homes or take out leases of whatever length suited them. Very few chose to buy. Apart from that, their biggest immediate challenge was to replace the rest of the community infrastructure. The only shop was housed in a leaky corrugated iron shack. The tearoom and craft shop by the pier, catering for visitors, were also falling apart. At last HIE came in with funding support to build An Laimhrig, which includes a tearoom, a shop and post office, a craft shop, an office for the Trust's only full-time employee, Maggie Fyffe, and toilets and shower facilities, popular with passing sailors. A trading subsidiary owns and manages An Laimhrig. Sensibly they decided to draw on the skills of their community to build it. That led to the creation of a construction subsidiary which has since raised the money to renovate five houses on the island and do improvements on two more.

But the biggest bugbear for the people of Eigg from way back has been how to power their homes and businesses in a predictable, affordable way. The island has never been connected to the National Grid and was never likely to be. Eddie Scott, who moved to Eigg from Ardross, near Dingwall, in 2005, is blunt about the consequences. To power his generator at his croft in Cleadale on the other side of the island, it used to cost him £150 a month to bring in a barrel of diesel. Providing his generator was working that would give him up to six hours of power a day. Now Eddie is one of seven part-time members of the maintenance team at Eigg Electric, the community's own island-wide grid, powered by four small wind generators, three hydro schemes and a growing array of photo-voltaic panels, all backed up by 96 storage batteries, controlled by inverters, and two stand-by generators. It cost some £1.6m, with funding raised from a variety of sources.

'I now get 24-hour power for a tenner a week,' he chuckles. Later the island's doctor told us his bills for his surgery had fallen from £600 a month to £250 a quarter. The only restriction is a cap at any one time of 5kW for households and 10 kW for businesses. Each has a small monitor to tell them when they're getting near their limit. The system, as currently designed, is expected to supply 90 per cent green power. Since it was first switched on, in February 2008, it has managed to exceed that target one year and fell a little short in two others. But, even at that, it is way ahead of anything being achieved on the mainland by the big commercial utilities that turned their backs on supplying Eigg for so long.

Later in the day Eddie took us on a tour of parts of the system. Up to the four 6kW turbines on high ground beneath Eigg's pitchstone Sgurr, by way of the central control house and battery store. The biggest generator on the system is the 100kW capacity hydro scheme at Laig. The solar array, which currently has a capacity of 30kW, may be expanded in future. Certainly, the day we were there the temperature had hit 33°C, hotter than the Bahamas. Arguably the crowning achievement of the Eigg system is the 11 km of high voltage supply cable, taking round-the-clock electricity to every corner of the island, all of it buried underground, to avoid spoiling Eigg's breathtaking views. The grid avoids roadsides (to ensure no way leave need be paid to the council) and navigates its way around near-surface rock formations.

Much of the credit for that goes to one man, John Booth. With his wife Christine, John chose to retire to Eigg when they bought one of the houses from the Trust. Initially, says Maggie, he wasn't convinced the electricity scheme would work. But now, having walked the length and breadth of the island exhaustively to work out where that underground grid could most cost-effectively go, all in a volunteer capacity, he is one of the scheme's strongest advocates and a director of the business. It's a telling example of how people, given more control over their own destiny, can achieve remarkable things.

In similar vein, Eigg has cracked another perennial complaint in many parts of rural Scotland. The lack of cost-effective, fast internet access. A string of older initiatives had under-delivered, especially in places like Eigg with no reliable electricity supply. Since the arrival of the island grid that problem has gone. And newer, satellite-based systems became available. But these were expensive and still rather slow.

Eddie Scott told us he was paying £23 a month for a 0.5Mb service that was proving rather unreliable. Then, in 2010, an Edinburgh university professor who had been experimenting with a much faster, wireless-based distribution system for broadband at Loch Hourn, further up the Sound of Sleat, came to Eigg. Using an experimental link into Mallaig High School, he showed what could be done. The school, like all public buildings in Highland Region, is linked into a high-speed trunk network. Getting access to that would have allowed the HebNet system that Eigg was developing exploit much more of the 50Mb speeds of which it is capable. But, even after negotiations, that particular broadband motorway remains closed to them. So instead HebNet is currently linked wirelessly into the ADSL lines at the telephone exchange in Arisaig. Even with that service Eddie is now paying £15 a month for between 6 and 7Mb, a deal a lot of city dwellers would envy.

There's plenty more to be said about what a liberated Eigg is now achieving. Its forest business, boosted by the trees that came down in the gales of 2011/12. A £300,000 prize in 2010 in a NESTA competition to promote community innovation on reducing carbon dependency. The newer businesses that are springing up, like the 24-bed luxury hostel and outdoor centre at Glebe Barn or the young couple trying to turn the former laird's house into an environmental education centre as well as a home for them and their three children.

Before we left we met Alastair McIntosh and his party of Indonesian planners again. They had been staying at Glebe Barn. Some of them had even found it difficult to sleep in this unexpected Scottish heat wave. More importantly, they had been deeply impressed, as we had been, by what had been achieved on Eigg so far. Eventually we boarded the *Sheerwater* again and headed back to Arisaig, for a shower, a meal with Neil and Eileen, and a chance to reflect, with them, on the lessons we had learned travelling our sunkissed new road.

To Knoydart Where Our New Road Ends. . .
for Now

WE SPENT a relaxing evening at Grianan swopping experiences of the West Highlands with Neil and Eileen, looking
out across Arisaig's boatyard to Eigg's darkening Sgurr twelve
miles away. And the sun set on another remarkable day, Next
morning we got up in good time and had some breakfast
before Neil kindly drove us back up the road to Mallaig and
the final stop on our journey.

There is no road, old or new, connecting Inverie on the
northern shore of Loch Nevis to the outside world. We were
catching a Seabridge ferry service to this, the largest of the
remaining settlements left on the great Knoydart peninsula,
which lies between Loch Nevis, at its southern bound, and
Loch Hourn, further north. All the others disappeared at the
time of the Clearances, when around 500 were shipped off
to North America. One of the other parties on board had
commissioned a detour around Glas Eilean, at the mouth of
the loch. Green Island is a bird sanctuary. The first of the
season's Artic skuas had already arrived and were busily

coming and going in search of fish as their breeding season commenced.

As we sail on into the loch itself we are soon confronted by a tall white statue, standing on a stone plinth on a rocky outcrop, looking out to sea. It is an image of the Madonna, with arms outstretched, and was put there by one of Knoydart's previous owners, Colonel Sir Oliver Crosthwaite-Eyre. The Eyre in his surname is the same family that helped found the Eyre & Spottiswoode publishing house. The colonel was a Royal Marine who, after World War II, turned to politics, representing the New Forest as its Conservative MP from 1945 until he resigned in 1968. He was married to the daughter of an Austrian baron who created the Salzburg music festival. It is said the face of Our Lady of Loch Nevis bears more than a passing resemblance to her ladyship's own. The original was apparently carved in stone, but proved too heavy to manoeuvre onto its isolated resting place. So a mould was made and a lighter, synthetic version is what greets us. Some locals call it the Plastic Mary.

The ownership history of Knoydart throws up some surprises. Earlier we noted that William Baird brought coal mining to Twechar. For much of the second half of the nineteenth century his brother James (of Cambusdoon in Ayrshire) owned Knoydart. But in the twentieth century self-made Victorian coal and iron barons gave way to a very different kind of laird. Some were to weave a story every bit as depressing as that of Eigg's more dubious custodians.

The colonel bought it in 1952 after Lord Brocket, who had owned it since 1933, decided he had had enough. Brocket was a Nazi sympathiser who travelled to Germany to celebrate

Hitler's birthday just months before the outbreak of the World War II. And it was on Brocket's watch, in 1948, that the Seven Men of Knoydart, all ex-servicemen from the area, staged the last land raid on Scottish soil, asserting their right to farm a small patch of their native turf. Brocket took them to court and won. In 1972 the colonel sold to Major Nigel Chamberlayne-Macdonald , who filled a whole series of ceremonial roles in the Royal household. Both the colonel and the major attempted improvements to the estate, notably building the village hall at Inverie, a pier and a hydro scheme to power the village. But in 1983 the major sold all 55,000 acres of the Knoydart estate to a polo-playing Surrey-based property developer, Philip Rhodes.

By common consent Rhodes did some good things during his tenure. But his main instinct was to break the vast estate up, selling it off in various parcels, until Knoydart itself, the land around Inverie, was reduced to 16,500 acres. Thanks to his asset stripping the John Muir Trust was able, in 1987, to buy its first estate, at the northern coast of the peninsula, including the last Munro on the mainland, Ladhar Bheinn. Rhodes himself still retains a parcel of land further up Loch Nevis, opposite Tarbet, where the musical theatre producer Sir Cameron Mackintosh has his Nevis Estate.

Knoydart itself changed hands several times in the 1990s. Indeed, for the locals, it was hard to know who or what vehicle was in control at any particular time. In 1993 Rhodes sold it to Reg Brealey, chairman of Sheffield United football club and of Dundee-registered and UK stock market listed shell company, Titaghur Jute. Clearly the trade that brought some of the women to the centre we had visited in Dundee, just days before, had grown some remarkable tentacles. And, shades of that bogus naval commander who once owned Eigg, Brealey had wanted to use Knoydart as a boot camp for delinquent youngsters. It never happened.

Then, in 1998, it emerged that Knoydart was controlled by Stephen Hinchcliffe, a one time Renault car dealer from Sheffield, who had, like Brealey, owned a slice of the Blades. He had become a flashy retail entrepreneur, whose Facia empire controlled high street brands like Trueform, Saxone, Red or Dead and Sock Shop. He even flew around in a helicopter he'd bought from Gerald Ratner. But in 1996 Facia had collapsed with debts of £70m. Two years before the community of Knoydart discovered he was their Laird, Hinchcliffe was already the subject of a Serious Fraud Office investigation. In 2001 and again in 2003 he would go to jail for fraud. Back in 1998 Knoydart Peninsula, Hinchcliffe's vehicle, had gone into voluntary receivership. The main creditor now was Bank of Scotland, but the bank was reluctant to consider a community buy-out.

These extraordinary events had unsettled the small number of people left in the community. As on Eigg, staff on the estate were no longer being paid. But preparations for responding to this kind of crisis had been going on for some time. In 1997 Highlands and Islands Enterprise, now with a community land unit at the insistence of the incoming Labour government, had been looking closely at what was happening in Knoydart. That led to the creation of the Knoydart Foundation that same year. Apart from residents, the foundation was supported by a number of other groups. One was the Chris Brasher Trust. Another was the John Muir Trust, the conservation charity named after the man whose statue we had passed in Dunbar High Street on day one of our journey. A third backer was Kilchoan, the neighbouring estate, important because the loch that feeds Knoydart's hydro scheme, lies on its land.

From across Loch Nevis there was an attempt by Cameron Mackintosh to buy Knoydart from the receiver and lease it back to the community for a nominal rent of £1 and a bottle of whisky a year. But this was a community that now wanted to control its own destiny. There had been a public appeal for support that raised around £150,000. But it would take five times that to clinch the deal. Contributions from the Brasher and John Muir Trusts, HIE, Scottish Natural Heritage and Mackintosh's charitable foundation put the target within reach. But again, as on Eigg, an anonymous donation of £100,000 sealed the deal. On March 26 1999, the Knoydart Foundation took control.

We had come to meet Angela Williams, the Foundation's development manager. 'Watch out for the goose when you come up to the house,' she'd warned. It still tried to take a bite at Alf's leg as we passed. A landscape architect who lived in Lancashire, Angela and her family arrived in 2001. She had never set foot in Knoydart before she came for her interview, but she and her partner had hankered after a move to Scotland's west coast and had been monitoring papers like the *Oban Times* for opportunities. What did it all feel like when she started work?

'At the beginning all our assets were liabilities,' she recalls. 'There had been ten years of neglect. There were severe voltage fluctuations on the hydro. When I came there were only a few computers and they weren't reliable.' The community was still coming to terms with the challenge it was taking on.

'One day you've got nothing,' is how Angela puts it. 'The next you're a landowner. A landlord. An electricity supplier. You've a deer herd to manage. Yet all the same legislation applies. It was sheer hard work.' In the first management accounts, the biggest income was interest from cash in the bank because the foundation had sold two properties on the estate. The other biggest income was rent. But there was a major refurbishment of the hydro scheme to fund. She was hardly in post before she was helping to assess tenders to upgrade the dam and pipeline and fix the turbine. The system was switched off for the best part of a year and, in the course of the work, the contractor went into liquidation. Luckily much of the work had been sub-contracted to someone else. He battled on, through horrendous weather, to complete the job. With hindsight, it might have been better to raise more money initially, and replace some of the old equipment. The work that was done was funded by Europe, HIE and the Knoydart Foundation.

Ten years on, with the community growing again, the system makes a surplus which is constantly being reinvested as well as paying back the loan to the Foundation. But the system is still posing challenges. It is rated at 280kW. But because of losses along the pipeline, at best it's producing 180kW. That still leaves spare capacity above the current average usage, but the margins are getting tighter. Knoydart Renewables, the Foundation's trading subsidiary which supplies the electricity, is exploring other options. Wind is difficult, given the terrain. There's the potential for another 100kw of run-of-river hydro on the estate. And they've also been exploring hydrogen as a storage system. 'We can't afford to go back to diesel generators, so it's a big challenge,' says Angela.

There are now 115 people living in Knoydart in nearly 70 houses. The other main subsidiary, Knoydart Trading, runs the popular 25 bed bunkhouse and sells merchandise, like Foundation T-shirts.

Although the only ways to get there are by sea or a walk of up to twenty miles from the nearest road ends, Knoydart is increasingly popular with adventure seekers, other tourists and customers of the remotest pub in mainland Britain. The Old Forge is renowned for its great food, real ales and folk music. It's also a place couples are coming to, with their friends and families, to get married. J and K were doing just that when we were there. We only know their initials. They were on a small notice board hung around the cairn commemorating the seven men of the land claim in 1948, in front of Inverie's village hall.

New businesses are also springing up. Like the pottery and tearoom where we enjoyed freshly-made prawn rolls and salad for our lunch. Knoydart welcomes between 8000 and 10,000 visitors a year now. A few days earlier, in the taxi in Glasgow to our bed for the night, our driver delighted in telling us the best fare he had ever had was from someone who had flown in late for a party in Knoydart and paid him a lot of money to drive, with minutes to spare, to catch the last boat leaving Mallaig for Inverie.

In the early days, the bunkhouse was another challenge. It was in a very poor state of repair when the Foundation took over. Set in old farm buildings, it was generating plenty of complaints. A big community clear-out was launched and a warden appointed. As the Foundation found itself with spare cash, it invested in new beds and carpet and later a new shower area. It sorted out the temperature in winter. And the warden,Izzie, has added some artistic touches.

'I cringe when I think back to what it was like,' says Angela. 'But now everyone loves it.' There is however a plan, when resources allow, to build a brand new one and turn the existing site into housing. That's another key issue for the Foundation. It inherited just five houses at the time of the buy-out, all of them in substandard condition. Two of them, including Inverie House, were sold. So, over the years were a number of plots for people to build their own homes. The Foundation isn't a housing association or a social landlord, but it has been restoring the houses it still owns, built an A frame timber house in 2002 and, more recently, won funding to complete three other homes for rent. That marked a community first.

There is one other housing issue. The Knoydart Foundation, which only exists today because it was able to exercise a collective right to buy the land for the community back in 1999, has no right-to-buy power written into its own constitution. Some think that power should be there, in the spirit of how the original buy-out was made possible. But others in this very special corner of Scotland think adding that power to the Foundation's articles would open the door to attempts to buy their houses. That tension – between holding strongly to the principles under which this community came into being, while encouraging others to come and join its continued growth and prosperity – remains unresolved.

Meanwhile the Foundation has another big responsibility. It has more than 16,000 acres of land to manage on which there are only six miles of tarmacked road. There are red deer and wild goats on the land. If habitats are to be improved the deer have to be culled. And that means there is another business in selling the resultant venison. At first it was all sent to a game dealer on the mainland. But there is a compelling logic – in terms of bring more work into the community, reducing food miles and having another local product to sell to visitors – for trying to do much more of the processing locally. That process has started, but still has some way to go. There's also a market garden that's in community ownership. The days of unreliable computer links are over now that Knoydart has joined in to the HebNet wireless network pioneered on Eigg. It has spread to Muck and Rum too. Angela confirms Eddie Scott's view of it. 'It's so much cheaper and better than satellite,' she says.

Knoydart today is a diverse community. Although the oldest residents came from Harris in the 1960s, they are all incomers, except the children who were born here. They have come from all over the UK, from Germany, from France, from America and even New Zealand.

'Knoydart is now a very different place from what it was at the time of the buy-out,' Angela acknowledges. 'But it's important that we all know what being part of a land-based community foundation means. We can't get complacent. We need to understand where we've come from, if we are to move forward and meet the challenges that still lie ahead.'

It's a good way to bring our new road to an end, for now. We both could easily have spent a lot more time in many of the places we visited, including Knoydart. But it was time to go back to Inverie's pier and our ferry back to Mallaig. On this crossing we encountered another pod of Minke whales. Ewan, standing alone at the stern, while everyone else was straining to see one that had broken the surface ahead of us, looked down and witnessed the complete passage of another. Just a few feet below him, this whale made its stately way towards our port side, glided right under our boat, and was off into the depths.

Reflections at Our Road's End

THE NEW ROAD we travelled over eight successive days in May was only one of many such learning journeys we could have chosen. There are now literally hundreds of other community initiatives, on top of the fifteen we visited, to be found the length and breadth of Scotland. Some well established. Many at a much more formative stage. The growing development trust movement has clearly struck a creative chord across diverse parts of our land.

We both felt enriched by what we had seen and heard. And were still absorbing the many stories of determination and inspiration we had encountered along the way. However we had organised an early opportunity to test our initial reflections on others. Ewan has been development officer with the Ullapool Community Trust since May 2011, a post that is funded through HIE and LEADER. On the Sunday morning, after driving back from Mallaig to Loch Broom, we met over coffee in the Ceilidh Place to share our impressions with UCT's chair Susan Leslie, two other board members, Chrissy Boyd and Diane Campbell, and one of its members, Jean Urquhart MSP.

The Ullapool trust started in 2009 under the Powerdown initiative, conducting a thermal imaging survey of some local homes and a cluster of three public buildings, the village hall, the community owned swimming pool, Ullaspool, and An Talla Solais, its art gallery. The survey led to energy saving improvements to Ullaspool and the village hall. UCT also secured funding to install solar heating panels on the roof of the pool while part of Powerdown. A district heating scheme, using a biomass boiler, that would heat all three buildings is at an advanced stage of development.

By the time we made our journey UCT had conducted an extensive consultation exercise with its community, which stretches all the way from Gruinard to Elphin. Through a household survey, focus groups and an open day, it had refined a community growth plan, agreed in September 2012. The plan has six sets of priorties, covering housing and local services, transport, local food, young people and apprentice-ships, community assets, and renewable energy and sustain-ability.

Having defined its priorities, UCT is winning funding support to take some of them forward. For its community to become more sustainable in terms of energy use, the Trust now has funding for a second part-time employee to develop a locally-sourced log supply business. And it is recruiting another full-time person to develop its Pure Power for Lochbroom initiative, to help more households reduce their dependence on fossil fuel. Other issues like improved public transport and better broadband are also being addressed,

If our journey has taught us anything it is that, all across Scotland, a new mood is awakening. People at a local level

Ullapool

are increasingly frustrated at top-down solutions to life's myriad challenges. The slow pace of that kind of institutionally-driven change. The ever-present tendency to find reasons why things cannot be done. Officaldom's fear of opening the taps and letting local initiative and enterprise flourish. We met many people, over those eight days, who are instinctively entrepreneurial. But not in a let's-make-loads-of-money sort of way. These are a new breed of entrepreneurs, fired by an ambition to light fires of social enterprise down among the grassroots of communities, large and small. People who will rock the boat. Ruffle feathers.

However that kind of enterprising spirit isn't enough. For communities to take more responsibility for their own destinies requires an unbelievable amount of hard work and effort by all involved in the action. Not just the commitment of the small numbers of people trusts can afford to employ. Especially from the countless volunteers who are the primary engine of this growing movement. They give freely of their time and experience. For many it has offered a more rewarding retirement. But with the decline in a printed press, much of what they are doing goes largely unsung. Especially outwith their own community boundaries and certainly among those who have yet to hear anything about what community development initiatives are achieving. Despite the good work of Development Trusts Association Scotland and others, it often feels as if each community setting foot on this new road has to redraw, from scratch, the map that will shape its journey. There is plenty of information available on how to set up such an initiative from scratch. But for those who have attempted it, it can still feel like a very lonely, at times scary, experience.

This new road can be bumpy. We heard again and again how tensions and jealousies can suddenly erupt in the smallest community. Allegations that agendas are being hijacked by incomers or the green lobby. The most well-meaning proposal can sometimes stir up dissent, even resentment, among others in the community who do not see it as a priority or as something that intrudes on them. To minimise that risk, trusts must go out of their way to consult and report back to the communities they claim to serve. Accountability matters.

There are also tensions with the more rule and procedure bound world of local and national government. The bewildering array of grant funding and other support on offer, can sometimes feel like a minefield, not a helping hand. Much of it is short-term. There's lots of overlap and confusion. If central government sees the growth of the development trust movement as some kind of silver bullet, a way of rolling out reform of costly, existing delivery structures, like local government, in a time of increasing austerity, it risks killing the essentially bottom-up nature of this grassroots empowerment. What we found were lots of people who think the way we live is in a profound phase of transition. People who don't think we are going to get back to the way we were before the great crash. Any attempt to impose a top-down template on this movement would kill it stone dead.

Some of the initiatives we visited are already well down the road to replacing some of their start-up funding support with community-owned assets that will, in time, deliver a community-controlled revenue stream no longer dependent on grants paid out of general taxation or National Lottery funding. However not every community can tap into a

119

commercial wind-farm or buy a mature forest on its doorstep. But to prosper in the long term, we believe all trusts may have to turn themselves into social enterprises of genuine scale. We need to think much more radically about what assets communities might aspire to control. We have witnessed the benign impact on some of Scotland's remotest communities of the right to buy their own land. There must be scope, for instance, for towns across Scotland, currently witnessing the slow death of their town centres, to buy them and put them to new and more productive community use too.

As we travelled our new road we found inspiring examples of what is possible through bottom-up community action. Many of the initiatives we visited were in small towns and rural Scotland. Much of the thrust of public policy is on developing Scotland's cities as the real engines of future growth. We believe that more local communities within our great cities could benefit hugely by looking more closely at what development trusts in the rest of Scotland are already achieving. It will take both commitment and vision by many, many people, if all the natural communities across Scotland are to reclaim more control over their own destinies and be all they can be. A new road perhaps. But one all can aspire to set foot on. ☐

ACKNOWLEDGEMENTS

We would like thanks everyone we met, from Dunbar to Inverie, in the fifteen community initiatives we visited, for their willingness to make time to meet us and tell us their stories. Thanks also to Ullapool Community Trust for releasing Ewan from his duties as development officer so he could make this journey. Development Trusts Association Scotland helped make this book possible by providing funding towards our travel and subsistence costs. And Zoe van Zwannenberg, Jean Barr and Neil and Eileen Cameron were on hand, in Dunbar, Glasgow and Arisaig respectively, to offer us warm hospitality and a bed for the night along the way. To them all our warmest thanks.

ASSOCIATED WEBLINKS

Postcards from Scotland – information about the series and photographs Alf and Ewan took on their journey for *The New Road*.   http://postcardsfromscotland.co.uk

Sustaining Dunbar   http://sustainingdunbar.org

Twechar Community Action http://www.twecharhlec.org.uk

Fife Diet   www.fifediet.co.uk

Vivarium Trust   http://www.vivariumtrust.co.uk

A Thousand Huts Campaign – Reforesting Scotland
http://www.reforestingscotland.org/projects/huts.php

Fintry Development Trust   http://www.fintrydt.org.uk

Gal Gael Trust   http://www.galgael.org

Neilston Development Trust
http://79.170.44.121/neilstontrust.co.uk

Renton Community Development Trust
http://www.renton-cdt.org.uk

Comrie Development Trust
http://comriedevelopmenttrust.org.uk

Dundee International Women's Centre
http://www.diwc.co.uk

Transition Town Forres   http://www.ttforres.org

Sleat Community Trust   http://www.sleat.org.uk/

Eigg Heritage Trust
http://www.isleofeigg.net/eigg_heritage_trust.html

Knoydart Foundation   http://www.knoydart-foundation.com

Ullapool Community Trust   http://ullapoolcommunity.org/

Development Trusts Association Scotland
http://www.dtascot.org.uk

Centre for Confidence and Well-being
http://www.centreforconfidence.co.uk

OTHER TITLES IN THIS SERIES

The Great Takeover: How materialism, the media and markets now dominate our lives

Carol Craig

ISBN:978 1 908931061 £5.99

This book describes the dominance of materalist values, the media and business in all our lives and how this is leading to a loss of individual and collective well-being. It looks at many of the big issues of our times – debt, inequality, political apathy, loss of self-esteem, pornography and the rise of celebrity culture. The conclusion is simple and ultimately hopeful – we can change our values and our lives.

Carol Craig is Chief Executive of the Centre for Confidence and Well-being which she established in 2004. She is author of *The Scots' Crisis of Confidence* (2003 and 2011); *Creating Confidence: A handbook for professionals working with young people* (2007); and *The Tears that Made the Clyde: Well-being in Glasgow* (2010).

AfterNow: What next for a healthy Scotland?
Phil Hanlon and Sandra Carlisle

ISBN:978 1 908931005 4 £5.99

The authors of this visionary book look at health in Scotland and beyond health to the main social, economic, environmental and cultural challenges of our times. By setting out the 'challenges of modernity' and showing how we are living through 'a change of age', they examine the type of transformational change required to create a more resilient and healthy Scotland.

Phil Hanlon is Professor of Public Health at University of Glasgow, and
interested in some of Scotland's most intractable health problems.
Sandra Carlisle has been involved in numerous health and policy-related
research and evaluation projects including partnership working for social
inclusion and health inequalities and on the social determinants of health.

Letting Go: Breathing new life into organisations
Tony Miller and Gordon Hall

ISBN:978 1 908931 49 8 £5.99

Tony Miller and Gordon Hall explore the origins of 'command and control' approaches to management. They do so compassionately. The tragedy is that those that have fostered this approach in our workplaces have done so for understandable reasons. Most people who are given responsibility for an organisation want to do their best for the staff and those that the organisation serves. When things go wrong, as they always do, the reflex response is to create a stronger system of control. What the arguments in this book demonstrate is that effective management in a modern workplace requires the exact opposite. Leaders of effective organisations appreciate how their whole system works and demonstrate a willingness to 'let go' - to trust staff - to rely on intrinsic motivation rather than external controls.

[over]

Tony Miller is an electrical engineer by training. He retired recently from Robert Gordon University He was a member of the Deming Learning Network, based in Aberdeen.

Gordon Hall Gordon is the CEO of the Deming Learning Network in Aberdeen. He has identified with encouraging the search for knowledge in the context of management. He initiated a group known as the Unreasonable Learners, whose basic aim is to seek cooperation amongst the many forward thinkers across Scotland. Their web site is www.unreasonable-learners.com.